COSTUMES

OF

MOROCCO

This book was originally published
as Costumes du Maroc by Édisud,
Aix-en-Provence, in 1988

© Édisud, Aix-en-Provence 1990

Printed in France

ISBN 2-85744-419-2

JEAN BESANCENOT

COSTUMES
OF
MOROCCO

Preface by James Bynon,
School of Oriental and African Studies, University of London

Translated from the French by Caroline Stone

ÉDISUD
La Calade, 13090 Aix-en-Provence, France

TABLE OF CONTENTS

ACKNOWLEDGEMENTS

The publication of this re-edition of my collection of Moroccan costumes takes me back 50 years and I would like to express my sincere appreciation to all those, both Moroccan and French, who have helped me to bring to fruition a work which has had to overcome so many difficulties.

I also wish to thank the Moroccan Ministry of Cultural Affairs for its valuable support in agreeing to lend the originals preserved in the archives of the General Library of Rabat for their reproduction in this book.

Finally, my grateful thanks to the Moroccan Embassy in France who undertook to ensure the safe shipment of the documents from Rabat to Paris and their return.

Jean Besancenot

PREFACE

When, in 1934, the last dissident tribesmen on the fringes of the Sahara were finally brought under the control of the central Moroccan authority few could have foreseen the speed with which a society, which scarcely a generation before was still almost totally isolated in its traditional way of life, was to be precipitated headlong into a world dominated by the values of twentieth century western technology.

Of course many of the ancient institutions which were to be swept away in this process were long outmoded and in genuine need of replacement. The passing of these was inevitable. But there was also much of very real value in « the old Morocco » whose disappearance is to be regretted, facets of traditional life which charmed by their simple beauty, by their dignity and by their humanity, but which were unable to withstand the onslaught of imported cultural values. It should not of course be supposed that the demise of Morocco's traditional culture was the result of any deliberate plot on the part of authority, it was rather the simple victim of circumstances. Faced by the noisy throng of an ever expanding younger generation hungry for progress, like some unassuming and rather bewildered old man it just gathered its cloak about it and slipped silently away, scarcely noticed in its going.

But happily not entirely unnoticed, for there were some who witnessed these final stages of a disappearing world and who realised the value of what they saw. One such person was Jean Besancenot. Arriving in Morocco at a moment when, for the first time in its turbulent history every corner of this still imperfectly known country was fully accessible to the traveller, he set about recording in a series of dazzlingly beautiful yet thoroughly accurate images one of the more vulnerable aspects of Moroccan traditional culture. In the costumes which he has so faithfully recorded, as in the faces of their wearers, we are made acutely aware of that blending together of Orient and of Occident, of Europe and of Africa, which is one of the most striking features of Morocco. For here are to be found the ancient draped costume of the Mediterranean world, already so familiar to us from the vase paintings and statues of Classical Antiquity, the flowing Arab kaftan from the East, the magnificent festive dresses of the Jewesses of Morocco's northern towns, dresses which descend directly from those worn in the wealthy families of Andalusia before their expulsion in 1492, the richly decorated costume of Turkish origin favoured by the Sally Rovers... all these, like the shades of long dead actors filing slowly across a stage, recall in the most dramatic fashion possible successive episodes in the pageant of Morocco's history.

Confronted by these sixty magnificent plates, in which sitter and artist compete for our admiration, we can only express our thankfulness that, on the eve of its extinction, there should have been found combined in one man the foresight, the enthusiasm and the talent which would enable him to preserve for us, and for all future generations, at least a well chosen sample of one of the most fascinating expressions of Morocco's unique traditional heritage.

James BYNON
School of Oriental & African Studies,
University of London.

7

PUBLISHER'S NOTE

The orthographic forms of the Maghrebi Arabic and Berber words in the text have been preserved exactly as printed in the original French edition. They represent the impression made on the ear of the author and noted down by him at the time of his investigations and as such constitute an important record. Their value to the scholar would be largely lost if they were to be «corrected» in the light of more recent studies of the North African dialects or of their etymologies in the Classical language.

INTRODUCTION

More than fifty years have passed since I arrived in Morocco for the first time, filled with the desire to record its costume and its ornaments.

My attitude was that of an artist, draughtsman and painter, working in the service of ethnography, using an approach which I had already tried out in the course of studying regional dress in Europe. I, therefore, proceeded to make extremely detailed drawings of sixty costumes and was determined that it should provide as complete a visual record as possible, while stressing the aesthetic quality that a garment lends to its wearer.

What first struck me when I examined the range of Moroccan costumes, was the juxtaposition and sometimes the mixture of traditions inherited from the Graeco-Roman world perceptible in the countryside and the Middle Eastern element — which appears from the VIIth century, the beginning of Islamization — visible in urban dress. This is so, for example, in the case of that very ancient type of clothing, drapery. The variety of materials, combined with the often complex ways in which the draping is carried out, led me to round out this graphic description with a series of sketches illustrating the successive stages in the draping process, which vary from group to group.

In the rural areas, each type of dress represents a tribal identity. Now, at the time at which I carried out this study, the tribal structures were still very much alive and very clearly differentiated, particularly among the people of Berber origin, a group which is generally considered to constitute the original native stock of the region.

The festive clothes of the townsfolk bear witness to the richness of those elements which derive from the refined Arab traditions of the Middle East.

Finally, the study of certain groups of Jews, very much an ethnic minority in Morocco, made it possible for me to draw attention to the existence of some particularly interesting costumes — their simple examination makes it possible to distinguish the elements indicative of the two great sources of immigration of this people: Palestine and Andalusia.

As regards ornaments, it was not possible for me to illustrate them in detail in view of the scale of the costume plates, where they are only suggested in outline. For this reason, I have dedicated several pages of sketches in the appendix to the most typical of the jewels and other costume accessories.

I have frequently been questioned on my method of work. To tell the truth, it mostly consisted of adapting myself ceaselessly to the very varied situations in which I found myself. I tried to give as complete a commentary as possible of the costumes which I saw in a given place at a given time — between 1934 and 1939 — rather than imposing a previously established plan of work on a largely unknown reality.

Very naturally, I decided to give preference to the most beautiful costumes, or at least to the most representative ones.

At this point, I would like to take the opportunity to acknowledge the very precious help lent me by my friend George Spillmann, who gave me the benefit of his vast knowledge of the history of the indigenous peoples and their distribution.

In these regions, which few outsiders had visited, it was not surprising that my enquiries about clothing — an aspect of people's private lives — met with difficulties.

Furthermore, I was a foreigner, male and non-Muslim, all handicaps when it came to studying costume, and especially that of women. Patience, tact and discretion gradually enabled me to obtain the elements of information which I needed for my study. In the rural world, the welcome given me varied very much from tribe to tribe. The great reserve of certain groups contrasted with the very convivial hospitality of others. This was the case, for example, among the peasant women of the Middle Atlas, who normally went unveiled and were extremely cooperative. In the far south, I have pleasant memories of my stay with the harratines. The *hartaniat*, cheerful and elegant in their remarkable draperies, provided me with extremely patient models. Each stage of my journey had its elements of surprise. In some cases I could work at leisure, drawing and painting and collecting ample information. At other times I was forced to make do with a few sketches and some snaps taken in a hurry. Have I made a complete inventory of the costumes which in Morocco are so varied? Certainly not, if only because events at that particular point in time made it impossible for me to extend my research into northern Morocco. Nevertheless, when I returned to Paris, the interest of my work was recognized. The publishing house « Horizons de France » agreed, in 1939, to produce a luxury edition: 300 copies with 60 loose plates representing the costumes in facsimile by means of the Daniel Jacomet process. I was then asked to produce explanatory texts to accompany my gouaches, which were arranged according to the ten great population groups.

This luxury edition, published in 1942, was a success and, today, I am happy to recall that His Majesty Mohamed V did me the honour of being one of the first subscribers.

Subsequently, various people interested in the subject have expressed a wish that a reprint accessible to a wider public might be produced. The past decades have seen an increased interest in ethnology, while at the same time many traditional cultures have vanished into the general standardization of ways of life. In Morocco, most of the costumes have completely vanished, as has the jewellery, which I recorded in a series of drawings published in 1953.[1]

Lastly, the precariousness of this cultural inheritance has been aggravated by the lack of information on the vernacular, since the various Berber languages are exclusively oral. This re-edition reproduces all the illustrations. On the other hand, a number of the accompanying texts have been brought up to date, and I have endeavoured to round them out by adding all the information that I have been able to collect in the course of my visits to Morocco. Something about which I care deeply is that my work be well-received and considered by the younger generations of Moroccans as a contribution to the knowledge of their very rich cultural heritage.

Jean BESANCENOT

---

1. *Bijoux arabes et berbères du Maroc*, Ed. la Cigogne, Casablanca.

Plates
of Costumes

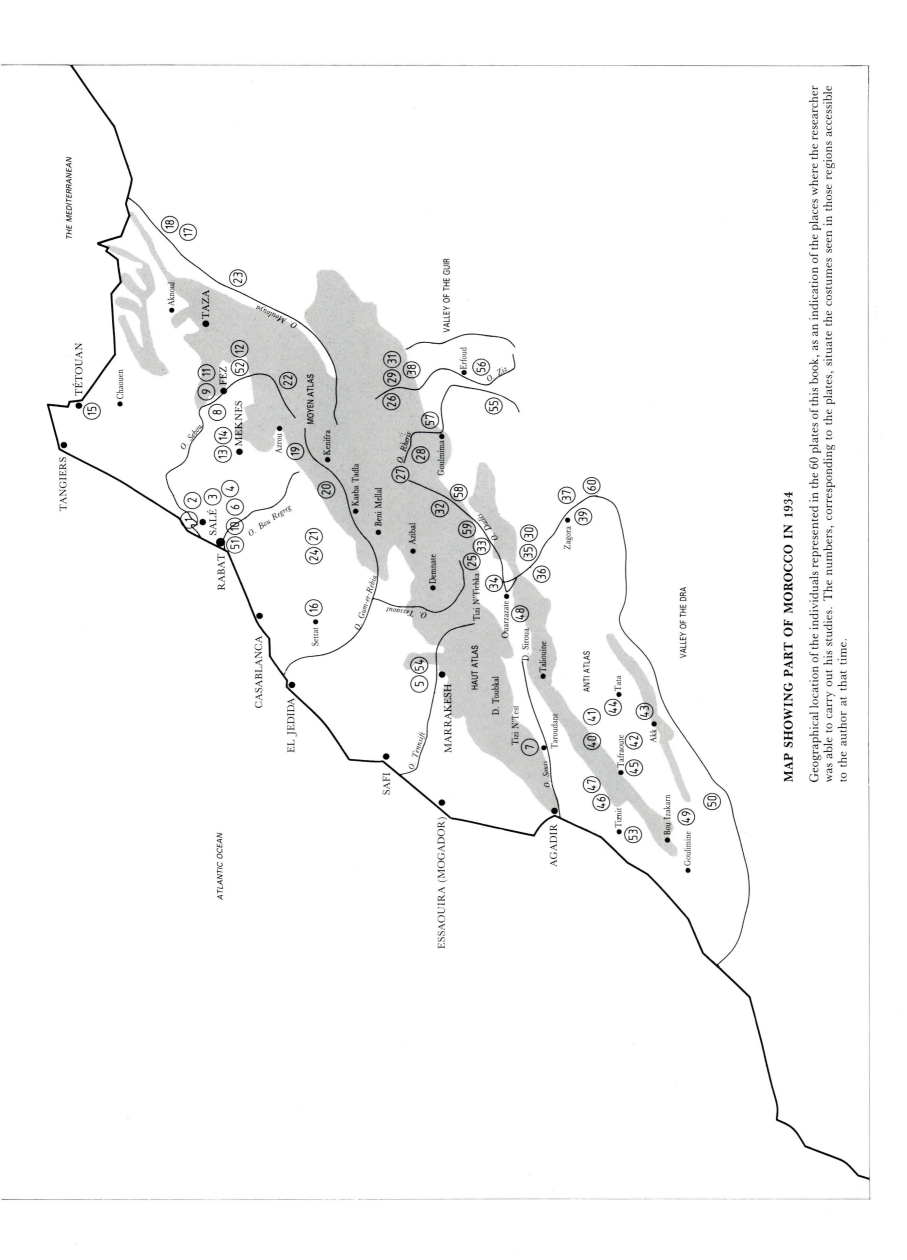

MAP SHOWING PART OF MOROCCO IN 1934

Geographical location of the individuals represented in the 60 plates of this book, as an indication of the places where the researcher was able to carry out his studies. The numbers, corresponding to the plates, situate the costumes seen in those regions accessible to the author at that time.

TABLE OF PLATES

THE TOWNSPEOPLE

THE CHAOUÏA

THE PEOPLES OF NORTHERN MOROCCO

THE MOUNTAIN TRIBES OF CENTRAL MOROCCO

2

3

6

7

11

14

15

19

21

23

4

33

38

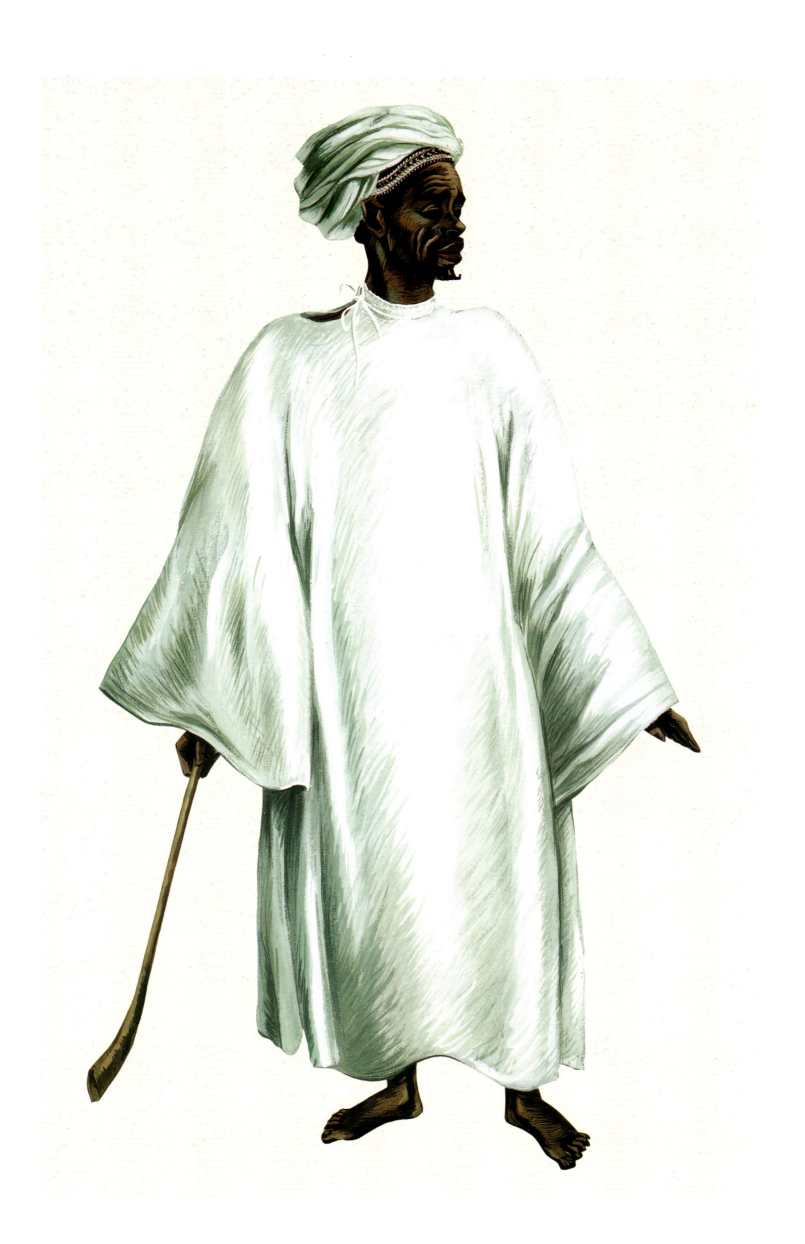

45

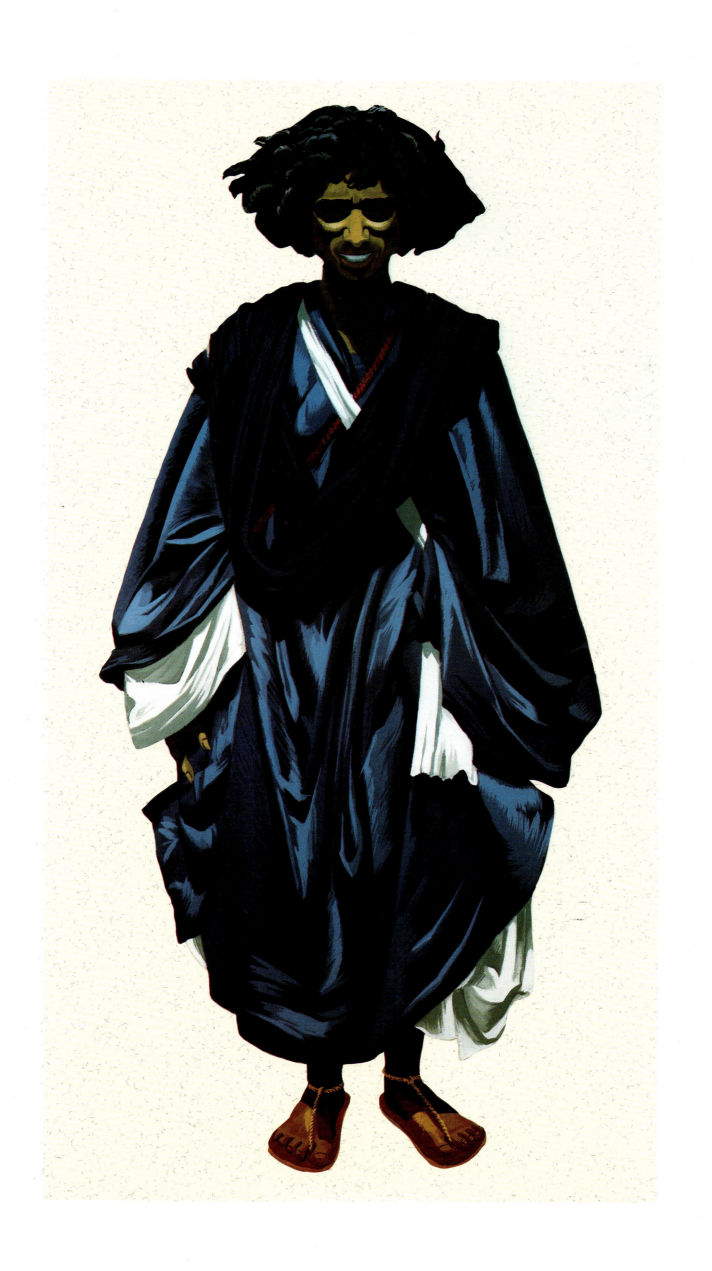

51

53

56

60

THE TOWNSPEOPLE

When I arrived in Morocco in 1934, no census of the Moroccan people had yet been taken. It is estimated that at that time the urban population represented about 15% of the inhabitants of the country. Faced with the problem of their rapid increase in size as a result of modern development, it was decided that each Moroccan town, each *médina*[1], should remain in its original state and that a new centre should be built outside the urban limits. This was a wise measure which allowed each Moroccan town to preserve its own special character. Among the most important towns, Marrakesh, Rabat, Meknes and Fez hold the rank of «Imperial Cities». The Sultan and his court spend part of each year in them, on visits dictated by protocol.

Only four towns, Fez, Rabat, Salé and Tétouan are what is called *hadria*, that is to say truly urban, the others being considered Berber. This distinction is based on the origins of their populations. Many of the inhabitants of Fez came at an earlier period either from the ancient city of Kairouan, founded by the Arabs in 670, or from the Muslim cities of Spain. Similarly, Tétouan, Rabat and Salé are proud to count among their numbers many families originally from Malaga, Seville, Cordoba and Granada, who were driven out of these places after the Catholic reconquest of Spain. The *hadria* towns have thus, more than any of the others, been deeply influenced by the brilliant civilization of Moorish Spain. It is to these immigrants of refined and polished habits that they owe their urban and educated character.

Most Moroccan towns were founded by Sultans who wanted to mark the grandeur of their reigns in a durable fashion, by creating either a capital or a fortified encampment designed to dominate a region of vital importance, or sometimes a port, whose commerce would then be under their control.

Fez was thus founded by Moulay Idris II in 808 A.D.; Marrakesh by Yusuf ibn Tashfin, the first Almoravid ruler, in 1060; Rabat by Abu Yusuf Ya'qub al-Mansur, the third Sultan of the Almohad dynasty (1148-1199). Meknes, the ancient fortress of the Meknassa Berbers, owes its present day splendour to Moulay Isma'il the Alawi (1672-1727); Mogador was the creation, in the XVIIIth century, of the grandson of that great ruler, Sidi Muhammad ibn 'Abd Allah ibn Isma'il, who had the plans drawn up by a French architect. Tiznit was built in the last years of the XIXth century by Moulay Hasan the Alawi, to keep a check on the Souss and the Anti-Atlas.

Intellectual activity was always the prerogative of the *hadria* towns, above all Fez, which, because of the importance of its élite, deserves the name of capital of Moroccan thought. The town which Moulay Idris II founded is proud of its ancient

---

1. Words of Arabic and Berber origin have been quite simply transcribed in romanized spelling. Only the Arabic sound which corresponds to the Spanish *jota* has been indicated by *kh* (e.g.: *khelkhal*: anklet).

Karawiyin University, at which very traditional classes are given by venerable *oulema* (scholars) to several hundred *tolba* (students), who come from all over Morocco. Its *medersa* — kinds of colleges in which these *tolba* are housed — are justly famous for the beauty of their architecture. They were built in the XVIth century by the Merinid dynasty.

Rabat and above all Salé, the ancient corsair town, are equally proud of their long-established and cultured bourgeoisie and of their men of letters, who have always held an honourable place in the world of wit and learning. These towns rival Fez.

Each of the Muslim towns is a great market, a real economic capital of the region. The town-dweller is therefore a merchant or a craftsman, whose clients are the neighbouring tribes. Commerce is considered as a highly honourable profession, which members of the ancient aristocratic and religious families in no way feel to be beneath them.

Casablanca is a completely different type of city. Of recent creation, it is a symbol of Morocco's modernity. A vast modern port has been built on the site of the old port of Anfa, which has served to open up maritime routes and place the country in contact with the outer world for a busy import and export trade.

This is the business centre and has indeed cast a certain shadow on the interests of Fez, which was previously the commercial heart of Morocco. The merchants of Fez have, however, been well able to adapt to this state of affairs and it is often their old families that control the large-scale businesses in the new city of Casablanca.

Location and climate lend each town its particular character. Marrakesh, which lies in the plain at the foot of the Atlas Mountains, has gardens worthy of the Hesperides, pools and palm groves, which give it the feeling of an oasis. It seems in essence African, even Saharan. It is also a great caravanserai, where the settled people of the plains rub shoulders with the mountain Berbers and the nomads from the great deserts of the south.

Mogador, Safi, Mazagan, Casablanca, Rabat, Salé are essentially maritime towns.

Fez is unique, like nothing else. At one and the same time Oriental, Andalusian and Moroccan, she represents the intimate merging together of three civilizations. The beauty of her site is unparalleled. Nestling in a shaded valley, abundantly watered by springs comparable to those in the Vaucluse, she is, in Mr. E.-F. Gautier's felicitous phrase, «a probably unique miracle of adaptation to the conditions of the oriental state.»

Her ancient bourgeoisie is elegant, cultured, intelligent, deeply attached both to its traditions and to the Muslim faith.

Her craftsmen, organized into guilds and working in medieval souks, where they are grouped by trade, have always played a crucial role in the history of the arts of the Maghreb, because of their taste and their faithful preservation of ancient techniques.

A city of arts and sciences, a university city, a city made holy by its famous mosques and tombs, an important centre of craftsmanship and of commerce, an Imperial City, Fez is the most original and the most perfect of the Muslim cities of Morocco.

The clothes of the town-dwellers are very clearly differentiated from those of the country people. Nevertheless, as we will see, some basic items of clothing are common to the two groups. Even in this case, however, the outward appearance is not at all the same because of the difference in materials used, as well as in the way in which the garment is worn. It is this, in fact, which gives the costume of

Morocco its particular character. Simple and consisting of few components, the Moroccan nevertheless manages to give it a widely varying appearance. In this the art of drapery plays an important part. Even clothes which are cut and sewn are worn with the aim of producing aesthetic effects by means of pleasing folds. In this work, it has not been possible to illustrate all the varieties of drapery and I have had to limit myself to reproducing a few of the most typical forms in the plates devoted to urban dress. There are also some outline drawings showing the exact cut of the most important pieces of clothing among the appended sketches.

Plate I shows a Moroccan in urban dress. This consists of a *jellaba* and *selham* which together constitute, by and large, the most widespread form of dress. Both of these garments turn up again almost everywhere throughout the countryside with certain variations in cut and in the quality of materials used.

The *jellaba* (pl.: *jlaleb*) is a short-sleeved outer garment with a hood, slightly slit at the bottom, at the sides and in front. It may be of imported cloth (worsted or flannel), or of locally made woollen stuff, more or less thick and warm, depending on the season. It may be of any colour depending on individual preference. There is, however, for elegant and well-to-do men, particularly in Fez, a kind of fashion which each season introduces certain new colours representing the taste of the moment. White, however, always lends an aristocratic air to the wearer. The man-in-the-street more commonly wears a striped *jellaba*.

Several *jlaleb* are sometimes worn one on top of the other. This garment is very often worn carelessly, the front edge of the hood folded back upon itself, and this can be of the greatest elegance on a man who knows how to arrange the folds and turn back the hood over his fez or his turban.

The *selham* is also an outdoor garment. It is a very full, sleeveless cloak with a hood decorated with a large silk pompom, *bellouta*. It is open in front, but is closed over the breast by the *sder*, a sewn band about 15 centimetres long, reinforced by very firm stitching. The edges are trimmed with silk braid in the same colour. Moroccans wear the *selham* in a great range of different ways creating, with the greatest ease and the most perfect taste, skilful effects of drapery, by which each affirms his own distinctive style, and it is hard for the eye to discern the original shape of the garment. Often, as may be seen in Plate 1, it is simply thrown negligently over the shoulders. The hood then drops very low behind and one of the side panels is brought across from one shoulder to the other. The *selham* is, above all, intended to protect against cold and in winter is generally made of dark coloured cloth, black or navy. It is also worn in the summer by the most elegant of the town-dwellers, but it is then made from fine white woollen cloth.

The man in Plate 1 is carrying folded under his arm a small prayer rug, *lebda*, without which almost no well-to-do town-dweller would set out for the mosque. He is wearing a pair of the classic urban slippers called *belra*. This is the usual outdoor dress.

Let us now consider the other items of urban costume. The *tchamir* is a long shirt of white cotton with wide sleeves. These are held in by wristbands when the shirt is to be worn under a narrow-sleeved piece of clothing. The small stand-up collar, *randa*, closing at the side, is often trimmed with needle lace.

The *keswa del mahsour* (narrow-sleeved costume) is a suit composed of four elements: trousers, two waistcoats and a jacket. It can be seen in Plate 3. The *seroual* are a kind of trousers known throughout the whole of North Africa. They are cut very wide and drawn in at the waist with a cord or strip of cloth, *tekka*, embroidered at the ends. The legs of these trousers are tight above the calves and the seat hangs down very low behind. Of the two waistcoats, called *bdaiyat* (sing.: *bdaiya*), the inside one is buttoned, while the outside one is left open. The jacket, *mentan* or *mental*, has long narrow sleeves, slit from wrist to elbow and fastened with buttons. It closes with a single button at the front of the neck. It may be replaced by the *jabadouli*, a sort of long shirt of fine cloth with no collar, with narrow sleeves buttoned on the forearms. The *jabadouli* is slightly slit at the sides, completely open in front and fastened at the top, like the *mental*. Over all this a *foqiya* is often worn — a sleeveless over-garment of a light material cut wide at the neck. The *joukha*, another outer garment which may be worn over the *jabadouli*, is of fine woollen cloth; it is completely open down the front and is again held at the top by a single button. This is a fancy garment worn by the elegant.

In a general way, the *keswa del mahsour* is the dress of the merchants, of the well-to-do. It is for indoor wear and out-of-doors is always covered by the *jellaba*, except in the case of sailors, as we will see below.

The *qaftane* (pl.: *qfatène*) is worn especially by scholars and high-ranking officials. Inherited from the East, this basic item of clothing is a kind of long gown of fine cloth with wide sleeves and no collar. It is sometimes closed all the way down by a row of little round buttons worked in thread, or else opens only down as far as the waist, in which case it is called *qaftane farajiya*. The edges are finished in silk braid in the same colour. The *qaftane* is not only for men; it is also worn by women and then is richly decorated with braids and edgings and is often made from splendid velvets or highly priced brocades. This piece of clothing has undergone some major changes in cut in the course of the past century. The sleeves in particular, which used to be very wide and bell-shaped, are now tending to become as narrow as those of European clothes. On top of the *qaftane* is worn the *farajiya*, an over-garment of a light transparent material and of exactly the same cut as the *qaftane*. These two robes are held in at the waist by a belt, the *mdomma*, which is of the same shape as those worn by women, but more sober in its decoration, being simply embroidered in a single colour of silk on leather. Plate 4 shows the *qaftane* and *farajiya* which together make up the classic costume of the *moghazni*[1]. On the whole the *qaftane* represents the old tradition, while the *keswa del mahsour* is the result of relatively recent developments.

The headdress of the younger townspeople consists of the well-known fez of red wool, known as *tarbouch*, decorated with a tassel of black silk, *choucha*. This headdress is of Tunisian origin and today is often worn on its own. Traditionally, however, bachelors and men from the middle income groups added a little white turban called *rezza*. Men of some importance may add to the *rezza* the *amama*, a long piece of muslin wound around it in a voluminous coil. The *tarbouch* may be replaced by a knitted skullcap, the *taguiya*. Furthermore, old men generally wear a small scarf of cotton or light wool, the *chane*, to cover the head and neck.

Yellow leather slippers known as *blari* are the normal town wear. They are worn with the back part folded forwards under the heel. There are several variants from the standard type: the *mséita* is thick and strong, made especially for walking; the *mbentra*, worn by scholars, has a thin sole and is of leather so pale as to be almost white; the *mkhousra*, the choicest of the slippers, is worn by important officials and is distinguished by the quality of the leather from which it is made and the elegance of its shape.

In the past, only old men wore knitted wool socks, *teqachir*, but trade with Europe has now made the wearing of mass-produced socks common-place.

(See the details of male urban dress in the pages of drawings appended to the text.)

---

1. The spelling of the words *Maghzen* and *moghazni*, which have passed into everyday speech, is determined by common usage. The *gh* should be pronounced like the Spanish *jota*.

In addition to the usual items of clothing, the more distinguished town-dwellers wear the *ksa*, as shown on the figure in Plate 2. It is a long piece of light woollen cloth, often striped across its width with bands of silk of the same colour as the background, measuring approximately 5 to 6 metres in length and 1.80 metres wide. It is draped about the body and over the head according to very precise traditional rules. In the past, most town-dwellers wore this draped garment; it was then made of heavy wool and was known as the *haïk*. Many rural Moroccans still wear it in this form, but the *ksa* of light open-weave cloth has, in the towns, remained the prerogative of high officials, who will wear no colour but white.

CITY NOTABLE PLATE 2

Over the *ksa*, a great *selham* of woollen cloth with a very open weave is worn, set on the shoulders and elegantly draped. Or, for official ceremonies, it is worn in a more severe fashion, slipped on quite simply over the head.

(See the appended pages of drawings for the different stages of draping the *ksa*.)

Above, I have mentioned the sailors' costume, the *keswa del bekhria*. This is simply the *keswa del mahsour*, but worn without the overgarment. It was the seamen's guild which introduced into Morocco the use of this dress of Turkish influence, transmitted by the corsairs of the North African coasts. In the past, it was worn exclusively by the *bekhria* (seafarers). The example shown in Plate 3 belonged to the chief of the seamen, *er-raïs d-essqif* of Rabat-Salé, Bou Hanini, who died some years ago. Magnificently decorated with gold braid on a black cloth ground, it was made in Tunis. It is very clearly reminiscent of the sumptuous costume of the Janissaries of the past. The usual *keswa del bekhria* is simpler, generally pastel coloured and decorated with silken trimmings in a stronger tone of the same shade. A broad belt of wool and cotton, or sometimes silk, the *kourziya*, completes the costume.

BOATMAN OF RABAT-SALÉ PLATE 3

Here we see the *qaftane* worn with a *farajiya*, the classic costume of the *moghazni* (servant of the *Maghzen*). The *moghazni*'s *farajiya* is split very high at the sides. On his head he is wearing a pointed *chachiya* of red felted wool made in Fez. It is decorated with a long tassel of dark blue silk, *choucha*, and is always worn without a turban.

THE SULTAN'S MOGHAZNI PLATE 4

The *moghazni* is never without his satchel, *chkara*, slung diagonally across his body on a decorative cord, *mejdoul*, nor his dagger, which is suspended at his other side in similar fashion.

In the past, all men carried daggers. In the towns, this practice is beginning to disappear, although in Marrakesh many men still wear them. The dagger can also add an extra touch of elegance to ceremonial dress.

The three most common types of dagger are, depending on the region, the *sboula*, with a straight blade, the *khanjer*, with a heavy curved blade, and the *koummiya*, with a long curved blade.

(For details of the daggers, see the appended pages of drawings.)

In the towns, the streets are enlivened by a certain number of popular entertainers, absolutely typical of all Moroccan towns: snake charmers, water carriers, acrobats, *guembri* players, etc. who could well provide material for a survey dedicated entirely to them. The *guembri* player has been chosen rather than some other regional type, because he makes it possible to show how people of the humblest condition are dressed — their clothes, like those of this person, are often reduced to a simple tunic, more or less patched.

GUEMBRI PLAYER PLATE 5

A camel hair cord, *khit*, is wrapped round his head. He comes from the Anti-Atlas, like most of his guild. A basket and a great satchel, *chkara*, decorated with shells, are the accessories carried by this member of the Imdyazen. These Berbers are, in Morocco, what the troubadours were in France in the Middle Ages, wandering from one community to another, through towns and souks, playing the old tunes and living on the generosity of their audiences.

TOWNSWOMAN DRAPED
IN THE HAÏK
PLATE 6

The outdoor costume of the Moroccan townswoman is extremely simple. All women wrap themselves in the *haïk*, a huge piece of woollen cloth, measuring roughly 5 metres by 1.60 metres, which conceals from view the shape of their bodies and their features. There are slight differences in the draping technique from one Moroccan town to another; explanatory drawings are to be found among the appended pages of sketches.

The *haïk* can be of fine wool, of coarse lumpy wool, *haïk mharbel*, or of wool and silk, *haïk chaara*. It will be noted in Plate 6 that the Rabat style of draping leaves only one eye visible. Also worth noting are the town shoes, which have a special shape, *rihiyat* (sing.: *rihiya*), and are black with a high back behind the heel.

The *rjlin seroual*, silk or cotton leggings, are tight at the knee and fall in accordeon pleats to the ankles. Just as the back part of the slippers, *rihiyat*, hides the heel, so do the *rjlin seroual* hide the ankle so that no part of the woman's body is visible. The tradition at Salé is identical and there, as at Rabat, the women display an excessive degree of prudishness.

Occasionally, in the past few years, some women have taken to wearing the male *jellaba*, with the hood bound tightly to the head by means of a headband, and yellow *blari* on their feet. This is a form of travelling dress only recently adopted by certain Arab townswomen.

(See the various stages of draping the city women's dress in the appended pages of sketches.)

TOWNSWOMAN OF
TAROUDANT DRAPED
IN THE TAMELHAFT
PLATE 7

All the *hiyak* of Moroccan townswomen are white, very occasionally with a blue or red stripe. The only exception is the black *haïk* of Taroudant, called the *tamelhaft*. In Taroudant, the *tamelhaft* is a compromise between the *izar* of the Berber women, which will be described later, and the *haïk* worn in the towns; it replaces on its own these two garments. The *tamelhaft* is made of black cotton and throughout Morocco the women of Taroudant are the only ones to veil themselves thus in black, as do their Muslim sisters in certain Tunisian towns.

The shoes seen here are the classic *chrabil* (sing.: *cherbil*), more or less richly decorated with embroidery of silk and gold thread.

(See the different stages of draping the *tamelhaft* in the appended pages of drawings.)

TOWNSWOMAN
WEARING
INDOOR DRESS
PLATE 8

No decent woman would go out into the town unless closely veiled in a *haïk*. Certain women of the aristocracy, the *chérifate*, do not in fact go out at all; they are not even allowed up on to the roof terraces in the evenings, as most Moroccan women are and, from the day they enter their husband's house, the four walls of their pretty flower-filled *riad* (the Moroccan patio) becomes their gilded prison. We will now see what a Moroccan woman wears at home. The townswomen wear the *qaftane* which we have already described but, in the case of women, this may be made of velvet, silk or brocade. Over the *qaftane* is worn the light *dfina*, a garment made of transparent muslin enriched by decorative woven patterns. The shape is the same as that of the *qaftane*, over which it fits like a halo. It is buttoned down to the waist and shows the *qaftane* through the slits at the sides and the front.

Formerly, only rich women could afford the precious materials woven with gold in Fez or Tétouan, or the costly silks imported from Lyons. Let us say once and for all that today artificial silks have replaced these fine-quality materials. In particular, shoddy Japanese artificial silk, in doubtful taste, has literally swamped the market, placing a pseudo-luxury within range of all purses. It must, however, be admitted that Moroccan women know how to make the best use of these bazaar silks and often skilfully combine the most unexpected colours. The brilliance of the light and the splendour of the everyday background allow daring effects which would be impossible in another setting and under less luminous skies. The subtle colours have been given the most suggestive names: *chems el achi* (sunset), *qémra* (moonlight), *qelb hjer* (heart of stone), *zbib* (raisin), etc.

The undergarments of a Moroccan woman consist of a shift, *tchamir*, or *tahtiya*, with a piqué, lace or embroidered collar. It is worn over drawers, *seroual*, which are in turn worn directly next to the skin. These have the same cut as the men's *seroual* but are often made from fine silky material. It is interesting to note that the townswomen, who are so accustomed to the most delicate embroidery work, do not themselves decorate the materials from which they make their clothes. They only embroider the collars and cuffs of their shifts, the narrow band, *tekka*, which is used to draw in the *seroual* at the waist and the ties of the *haïk*, as well as certain veils which they use to cover themselves on coming out of the bath. A new element has appeared in women's dress as a result of contact with Europeans: it is knitted underwear, called *qamija* or simply *el trico*, which is much prized by the townswomen.

Headdresses have undergone profound changes as the result of the arrival on the markets *(souks)* of large quantities of cheap silk stuffs. The shawls and head scarves made from ancient brocades no longer exist except in traditional ceremonial dress. Today, the normal head covering is a silk scarf with fringes called *sbniya roumiya* (Roman — that is to say European — scarf). It encloses the whole bulk of the hair, which is firmly held in place by a headband, *hrarz*. It allows a wide range of whimsical variations: the headdress called «chicken-style», *chedda el djaja*, because the fringes hang down at the sides like a hen's wings; that known as «fan-shaped», *chedda el mrouha*, because it spreads out very widely, etc. The rich scarf of silk brocade is known as *sbniya del fra* (scarf with a foliate pattern). Another is called a «scarf with hearts», *sebniya del qloub*, from the little heart-shaped gold ornaments which spangle it.

Shoes vary slightly in shape and decoration from town to town. The *chrabil*, strong slippers embroidered with silk and gold and silver thread, are the most common. The townswoman in Plate 8 shows the modern trend in female dress. The belt which draws in the waist of her *qaftane* and her *dfina* is the *mdomma*, similarly embroidered in silk and in gold thread. It is fastened in front with a buckle covered by an ornament in chased gold, *fkroune* (the tortoise). This, today, has replaced the high belt of silk and gold brocade, *hzam squelli*, which was formerly woven in Fez. The gold jewel on her forehead, the *taba* (seal), is a classic ornament possessed by all well-to-do townswomen. The gold hand hung about her neck, *khamsa*, which is well-known under the name of «Hand of Fatima», is a good luck charm meant to give protection against the evil eye. When it is very large, it is called *louha*.

The most usual necklaces are the *médja del jouher* of baroque pearls, the white colour of which is admired, and the *khit er rih* of gold louis. Some beautiful old necklaces which will be described below are, today, no longer in fashion. The bracelets, *dbalij* (sing.: *deblij*), come in a wide variety of shapes, ranging from the slender bands of gold, *slouk*, to the thick twisted torque, amusingly known as *taasser saboun* (washing being wrung out). One pretty type of bracelet has alternating ribs of gold and silver with the charming name of *chems ou qemar* (sun and moon). The wide bracelet of thin metal, delicately engraved and pierced, the *mkhrem*, is more modern. There are different kinds of earrings, *khras*. The most common are the large pendants, *mticha* (swings) worn by the townswoman in Plate 8. There are also the *allaqat*, supported by a slender chain attached to the headband, the great rings called *mfatel* and the *douah*, rings enriched with hanging decorations of gold, coral and precious stones.

Urban Moroccan women make up heavily: they outline their eyes with *khol*, emphasize the red of their lips and cheeks with *aker* (a vegetable dye) and sometimes rub their lower lips with *souak* (walnut bark). They also use great quantities of *henna* with which they decorate their hands and feet. Certain beneficial properties are attributed to these ways of ornamenting the body; in particular they are said to keep away evil spirits. We will see further on how the face is also painted in curious ways for certain ceremonies. A thick decorative cord with trimmings of gold thread, the *hammala*, is wrapped round the arms in a figure of eight to allow the women to adjust the length of their sleeves. This, in a broad and general way, is the dress of the townspeople. It is the result of a gradual evolution and is very different from the clothing of the past, the principal elements of which are to be found in the ceremonial dress shown in the following plates. Women's dress is continually being influenced by fashion. This always emanates from Fez, the great city whose harems are familiar with all the most subtle refinements. If this new kind of silk or that new pattern of muslin are a success in the most prestigious of cities, they can be sure to spread rapidly throughout all the other Moroccan towns, where the women have no greater ambition than to imitate the luxury of Fez.

(See the details of townswomen's costume in the appended pages of drawings.)

TOWNSWOMAN DRESSED FOR HOUSEWORK PLATE 9

When women do their housework, they generally pull up their *qaftane* and their *dfina*, tucking the corners of these garments into their belts. Their *seroual*, which hangs down rather low, is then visible and their postures are often charming. The dress worn for housework does not, in any case, exclude a certain chic and may include a fine quality *qaftane* and *dfina* in carefully matched colours.

The townswoman in Plate 9 is wearing the headdress known as «chicken-style», held in place by a headband, *hrarz*. On her feet she is wearing *qouaqeb*, wooden soles held on by a broad leather strap, which perform the role of little indoor clogs.

MUSLIM BRIDE FROM SALÉ PLATE 10

If changing habits have tended to make town clothes more uniform throughout the country, festive dress has, on the other hand, been preserved in its traditional form. This bride from the town of Salé is an excellent example.

Each afternoon throughout the week of the marriage, for about one hour, the bride, *arousa*, sits for all her friends to view her, dressed in traditional costume and a quantity of jewels. Other women who wish to come and admire her may do so also, for on this occasion, exceptionally, the house is open to all. The bride must of necessity wear a white *tahtiya* and a white *seroual* of new cloth, over which she wears her usual clothes. To these are added the garments peculiar to the marriage ceremony. The *arousa* in Plate 10 is wearing a *qaftane* of garnet-coloured velvet trimmed with gold braid which is in the style of the ancient *qaftane* of Rabat. It does not button and its sleeves are very wide. Since nothing in the bride's dress may be knotted (in order to avert any evil spell), the *qaftane* is worn without a belt until the seventh day of the ceremonies, *nhar es sebaa* or *nhar el hzam* (the day of the belt), after which the bride is considered to be fully integrated into her new status and out of reach of the *jnoune*, evil spirits.

The *izar del hrir* is a great veil of silk, its ends brocaded in gold, which completely envelops the bride. Her hair hangs loose. Her head is bound up in a long scarf of red silk with gold brocade ends, the *cherbiya*. A scarf of white cotton, *ched el biad* and a headscarf of thick red and gold brocade, *abrouq*, form the body of the high rigid headdress on which are attached several headbands of velvet, *hiyout*, covered with little baroque pearls. The largest, called *taj*, is also decorated with pearls, but has, in addition, five ruby and emerald cabochons. Two pairs of artificial plaits,

144

the *hiyout bes squelli*, hang down on either side of the face, covered by the *zraïr*, cascades of small pearls. In addition to the necklaces, *medaïj del jouher*, she is wearing the ancient gold *lebba* with nine richly worked pendants. The details of the decoration of this jewel, whose origins lie deep in the past, have varied over the course of the centuries. The oldest ones preserve medieval lines, the more recent ones approximate to modern jewellery in their very delicate, but insipid and characterless, chasing. The earrings are of the kind called *douah*. The handshaped ornaments *khamsa* and *louha* are hung about the neck. Under the slightly raised *qaftane*, may be seen on the right foot one of the *khlakhel* (sing.: *khelkhal*), anklets, which are generally hidden by the *qfatène* which overlap them. On her feet the bride is wearing thick embroidered *chrabil*.

Her hands are decorated with patterns of *henna*; they rest on little handkerchiefs embroidered in Rabat stitch. The complicated make-up of the face, peculiar to Salé and Rabat, is obtained by means of a red dye, *aker* and a special white substance called *bioud l'oujah*. It is intended to protect the bride from the evil influence of the *jnoune*. Only the *chérifate* disdain to use it, such high-born people having, it is said, nothing to fear from evil spirits.

The *cherbiya* and the *abrouq* represent an ancient style of cloth which used to be woven in Fez. Like the diadems, they are very valuable and only rich families possess them. But they are very willing to lend them to adorn brides from less well-to-do families.

The marriage ceremony takes place with certain variations of detail in each town and, similarly, the bride's costume varies. That of the bride from Fez is very peculiar and impressively steeped in tradition. The *arousa* is perched on several mattresses placed one on top of the other against the *haïti*, the piece of cloth or velvet, richly embroidered in gold which decorates the walls of the living quarters in Fez. The outline of her body is completely hidden under the mass of voluminous cushions placed on her knees and all around her. Only the head of the *arousa* emerges from the heaps of cloth which cover her. The *qosba del berkato*, a voluminous stole of thick gold brocade woven in Fez, is worn over the *qaftane*, which should preferably be green or pale blue, *daw es-sbah* (morning light). Its two wide panels of stiff cloth reach as far as the ground. The two side panels of a second stole come down a little less low. This last, the *qosba del rib*, is of embossed brocade from Lyons. Over this again is draped the *msilka*, a long piece of white silk, brocaded in gold along the edges. At the sides, two large pieces of red and gold brocade, also woven in Fez, the *kmam*, which as their name implies represent the sleeves, are pinned to the *haïti*.

The necklaces are not hung about the neck, but attached inelegantly to a rigid plastron, *bséta*, covered in velvet. These are the *medaïj* (sing.: *medja*), necklaces of fine pearls with a large clasp of jade, and the *lebba*. The latter is of solid gold, delicately chased, as is also the *taj*, which crowns the head of the *arousa*. These jewels represent the modern trend and, as has already been mentioned, differ from the shape and traditional character of the ancient pieces. The narrow black braid on the forehead with the green stone in the centre is the *selta*. The standard bunches of small pearls, *zraïr*, hang down on either side of the head, together with the *nouasi*, long strips of black satin, also worked with pearls. One can imagine the luxury of such a ceremonial costume which, together with its jewels, may well be worth a very considerable sum. It does not in fact, belong to the bride and there exist only a small number of them, the property of wealthy *neggaguéf* (sing.: *neggafa*), matrons who specialize in marriage ceremonies. They hire out the clothes, the jewels and their services as dressers for the duration of the celebrations. It would have

MUSLIM BRIDE FROM FEZ PLATE 11

been difficult to show the bridal dress of all the main towns in this work. Those of Fez, Rabat and Salé are the most typical.

(For details of urban jewellery, see the pages of drawings in the appendix.)

COSTUME OF A
HATTARA FROM FEZ
PLATE 12

The *hattara*, or guest of honour, called upon to take part in a ceremony, has a duty to be sumptuously dressed. For a wedding especially, at the hour at which the bride is displayed, the guests, richly dressed, are seated about the *arousa*, the most venerable closest to her, in order of importance. The *hattara* in Plate 12 is wearing a light *dfina* over a rich *qaftane* of embossed silk from Lyons. The headdress is adorned with the classic frontal, *taba*, and the *touij* (little *taj*), an ornament of solid gold with modern chasing, articulated along a single central hinge. The presence of birds among the decorative elements is to be noted: it is typical of the work of Jewish craftsmen. Her forehead is bound by a narrow frontlet decorated with small ornaments of chased gold called *ayacha*. The earrings are splendid *allaqat*. Around her neck are a necklace of pearls, *medja*, a little hand (*khamsa*) for good luck, and a sizeable necklace of pendants called *lbiba* (dimunitive of *lebba*), because it is lighter than the old-style *lebba*.

This *hattara* is wearing — and this is a relatively modern touch — the *hammala*, or decorative cord which is normally passed round the shoulders to adjust the length of the sleeves, slung diagonally across her body.

TOWNSWOMAN DRESSED
IN FESTIVE COSTUME
PLATE 13

All the great events of life are pretexts for celebration during the course of which the women can give free rein to their coquetry. Like weddings, circumcision is one of the events for which Moroccans wear their finest clothes. On this occasion the mothers may even dress again in the marriage costume. Here we see how the *izar del hrir*, which is also called *rlila*, is held in front of the shoulders by small fibulae, *bzaïm* (sing.: *bzim*). It may or may not be caught by the belt, but it is always worn very open at the breast so that it does not hide the necklaces.

The woman in Plate 13 is wearing a headdress which follows the ancient tradition in favour at Meknes. She wears the *taj dial sfifa*, a diadem of married women. It is placed on top of a brocade scarf from Fez, *sbniya hliwa*, the hair having previously been enclosed in two scarves. The headdress thus obtained is voluminous and the scarf of very stiff brocade, folded over on itself several times, stands very high. Around this headdress is wound an ornament of ostrich feathers, *tartor*, and from the temples hang two ornaments of silver and beads which, because of their particular shape, are given the name of *fnarate* (lanterns). These jewels are peculiar to Meknes and are not found in other Moroccan towns. Like the *hattara* from Fez, this woman is wearing her *hammala* slung diagonally across her body and from it is suspended the *tehlil*, or little silver box containing verses of the Koran. On her face are the *harquous* decorations mentioned above. The black colouring can be prepared in different ways (generally from oak-galls, *yegg*, and soot) and makes it possible to imitate the customary motifs used in tattooing — but without, however, preserving the curative and prophylactic virtues which the Berbers believe them to possess. It is sometimes replaced by small pieces of black paper cut out and stuck to the face.

The position in which this woman is standing is due to a curious custom. At the moment at which the barber circumcises her small son, the mother must place her naked foot on a horse's bit submerged in a large basin of water. She must also hold the ends of the reins between her teeth, while simultaneously looking at herself in a small silver mirror. This, it is said, is either «so that the boy will become a fine horseman» or «so that iron shall not prove fatal to him.»

This costume is the expression of a tradition which has today fallen into disuse and almost has to be reconstructed. Only a few elderly *chérifate* of Meknes still wear it; it will disappear with them.

FORMAL DRESS CALLED «OF THE MAGHZEN» PLATE 14

The high stiff brocade belt from Fez, *hzam squelli*, girds the waist. It may, as one can see, be very wide. When it is wound several times round the body, closely binding the waist and trunk, it serves to some extent as a kind of corset and the older women who were still wearing it until recently, claimed that they would not have been able to do without it. The elegant women of the younger generation find this ancestral custom absurd. They prefer the becoming little *mdomma* and it is now many years since the skilful craftsmen of Fez who wove these magnificent belts of silk brocaded in gold were forced to abandon their looms. Today, except in Moroccan antique shops, few examples of this sumptuous weaving are to be found. The *hzam squelli* is decorated at either end with long cords and pompoms, *hdoub*, which are knotted in front. It is worn over the *qaftane* and *dfina* of ancient cut, with wide sleeves. But it is, above all, the headdress which gives this form of costume its particular character and it is called the headdress «of the Maghzen» because it was used by the women of the pasha's house. Two little pads of material, the *dmouj* (horns), attached at the sides increase the width of the structure. The head is covered by a rich scarf *sebniya dial lmizane* (handkerchief of the scales), so called because, being made of a very heavy brocade, it was sold by weight.

A frontlet, *sebniya mkhazniya*, held the whole structure together. It was surmounted by a tiara of fresh flowers and one of the pleasures of the well-to-do women of the past was the frequent renewal of this natural form of decoration. They would pass their whole time tending their appearance, painting and scenting themselves, and would seek out flowers of the colours which went best with their complexions.

As well as the jewels already mentioned, the *tajera* (opulent) is also shown here. It is an ancient form of necklace composed of three big rosettes skilfully pierced with interlacing geometric forms; the technique varies slightly depending on whether the jewel was made by craftsmen of Fez or of Meknes. Also worth noting are the great earrings, *allaqat*, which are hung from the headscarf by a fine chain to help the earlobes support their great weight. Certain very old examples even had inside a little reservoir filled with scent, which fell a drop at a time onto the shoulders of the wearer. The dark colouring of the model chosen to represent the women of the pasha's house should not cause surprise. Many of the *chérifate* do indeed have a dark skin, as a result of very frequent mixed marriages.

Here is a second example of an ancient costume which is now almost never worn. It is composed of a vast *qaftane* with wide bell-shaped sleeves. The one shown in this plate is called «of Tétouan». It was in this town in particular that the velvet *qfatène* lavishly decorated with gold lace and braid were made. The velvet was generally violet or garnet red, more rarely green or pale blue. The braided decoration, comparable to that shown in Plate 3, is the result of the same Turkish influence. This woman from Tétouan is wearing the little belt, *mdomma*, chosen expressly so as to reveal as much as possible of the decoration on the *qaftane*. In fact, tradition would have required that with such a dress she wear the high belt, *hzam squelli*, whose use has in fact been preserved in Tétouan more than in the other Moroccan towns.

TOWNSWOMAN WEARING THE ANCIENT QAFTANE OF TÉTOUAN PLATE 15

The jewels and headdress include a number of elements already described; the *tajera* comes from Fez and is of lighter construction than that of Meknes. The head covering consists of the traditional *taj* covering two lengths of antique brocade: the square piece is called *abrouq*, the long scarf, *cherbiya*.

At present, there are very few elderly women left who still dress in this «ancient manner», even in a town like Tétouan which has preserved its traditions more than others.

THE CHAOUÏA

The suburbs and hinterland of Casablanca were once the province of Tamesna. The small town of Anfa, present-day Casablanca, was one of its main centres.

The Tamesna area, which is today a vast plain exposed to the Atlantic, suitable for cereal crops and generally speaking treeless, was, until the XIIIth or XIVth century, a vast maquis, very hard to penetrate. Berber populations, the Berhouata, inhabited this region in which travel was difficult, living in an isolation and security made all the more complete by the fact that the coast was inhospitable and did not lend itself to landings.

The Berhouata had been converted to Islam by the end of the VIIth century but soon turned to heresy. One of their leaders, Salah ben Tarif, proclaimed himself a prophet and in 742 A.D. set up a new doctrine in opposition to Islam. He then created a theocratic kingdom which was to succumb only in the XIIth century under the attacks of the Almohad dynasty.

The Berhouata were then cruelly massacred and for a long time the land remained with few inhabitants. Little by little, Arab and Berber elements settled there. The newcomers amalgamated with the Berhouata who had remained and formed new tribal agglomerations, which are known today by the name of Chaouïa. The forest and the maquis gradually disappeared and the country took on the appearance it has today.

The Chaouïa are rich. Their black and fertile soil and the maritime climate ensure adequate harvests each year.

The tribes abandoned stock raising and gradually settled down to live by cultivation of the soil.

In the hinterland, where the first plateaux rise from the plain and where the influence of the Atlantic Ocean is less felt, the Chaouïa still own large flocks of sheep.

Most of the plains which are close to the great Moroccan towns are inhabited by Arabs, or heavily Arabized Berbers. The clothes are much influenced by urban usage. More or less everywhere, well-to-do men wear the *jellaba* and the woollen *selham* under a variety of names and the cut of these varies very little from one region to another. The everyday dress of the peasants, herdsmen and labourers is a short plain tunic of coarse wool, *tchamir* or *kmidja*, closing at the shoulder, or the *qchaba*, which is also a kind of shirt of thick wool with or without sleeves and fastened on either side of the neck by a cord.

Another kind of dress worn in the Chaouïa country is draped and represents the ancient tradition inherited from the indigenous peoples. It was certainly more widespread before urban male clothing began increasingly to be adopted by the peasantry. This is the *haïk*, here worn by the Chaouïa man represented in Plate 16. It is a simple woollen blanket, 4 or 5 metres long, woven within the tribal area, in which the Chaouïa man wraps himself in the manner of classical drapery, throwing one end over his shoulder. The gesture is beautiful and the overall impression is

149

reminiscent of the noble appearance of the drapery of the Roman toga. The *haïk* may be worn over a shirt, but it is sometimes the only garment worn. That used by the Chaouïa is striped with broad bands of colour, red and orange predominating, and is highly decorative. It should be mentioned, however, that the old pieces woven before the import of aniline dyes are very much superior in quality to the *hiyak* woven in this area today.

The Chaouïa women, like most of the women of the plain, wear Berber dress mixed with elements borrowed from the townswomen's costume, which somewhat corrupts the true expression of the rural tradition. It is only to be expected that the nearness of urban centres and the possibility of buying goods easily in the town markets *(souks)* should have encouraged this mixture. It will, therefore, be no surprise that I have deliberately avoided showing costumes worn in those parts of the plains which are close to the towns; they would add nothing to our knowledge of the subject. We will find Berber dress in its most original form in the areas which lie far from the great centres and especially in the mountain regions.

(For the different stages of draping the *haïk*, see the appended pages of drawings.)

THE PEOPLES OF
NORTHERN MOROCCO

The mountains of North Morocco are inhabited by people of Berber origin. While the western group, the Jbala, are heavily Arabized and speak Arabic, the eastern ones, the Riffians, have remained faithful to the old Berber dialects.

The statistics which claim that more than half of the population has brown hair and light-coloured eyes do not shed very much light on the mixtures of populations which must have taken place. What is quite clear is that the ancient indigenous stock has succeeded in assimilating all the changes. Between 1934 and 1939, due to the political and administrative division of Morocco, it was not possible for me to observe and therefore to describe, the Berbers of the Rif mountains. Therefore, a Riffian of the Gzénaïa and a man of the Meknassa will be used to illustrate this chapter.

The Meknassa near Taza keep a very low profile, despite the fact that their past was an extremely glorious one. In the Xth century of the Christian era, they established a powerful confederation and founded the town of Meknes. Their chief, Musa ibn al-ʿAfiya, destroyed the Idrisid dynasty and had himself proclaimed the Emir of Fez. He allied himself with the Shiʿa Fatimids who were then reigning in Tunisia, Tripolitania and Egypt, and in their name fought the Umayyads of Spain, then at the height of their power.

All this greatness collapsed in the XIth century under the attacks of the Almoravid dynasty, also Berber, which originated in the Western Sahara. The Meknassa were pitilessly slaughtered and in our own times exist only as a small group, heavily Arabized.

Men's costume, which used to differ from tribe to tribe, is tending to become increasingly uniform. The brief, but very evocative, descriptions by Charles de Foucauld in his *« Reconnaissance au Maroc »* are of a kind which give rise to all kinds of regrets in a painter-ethnographer who came to Morocco too late to observe certain very characteristic details which have vanished today. « If », writes this celebrated explorer, « dress is unvarying in the cities, it is quite the reverse in the countryside. At every turn, I see it change. As I go along, I shall describe these differences — they are such that one can tell from which region a Moroccan comes by his dress and arms. » And throughout the marvellous account of his journey, here and there the author gives an account of the nature of the clothes and above all the weapons of the tribes through which he passed. If the clothes are now tending to become more uniform, the ancient weapons have completely vanished. The most beautiful enrich museums, or else belong to collectors.

It is, therefore, more or less impossible, without entering the dangerous field of reconstruction, to show the Berbers in the warrior's outfit which was so dear to them last century. Nevertheless, it is perfectly true that one still meets a certain

A MAN OF THE MEKNASSA PLATE 17

151

number of male costumes which retain a very interesting local character and this book includes a number of plates showing the most typical of them.

The man of the Meknassa in Plate 17 belongs to a type very commonly found in North Morocco. The striped *jellaba* which he is wearing, constitutes a transitional stage between the townsman's *jellaba* and the very short *jellaba* of the mountain people of the Rif. The brown burnous, worn quite simply thrown across the shoulders, is the *haïdous*, the cloth being more rustic than that of the Arab *selham*, because it is largely woven of goat's hair.

On his feet, this man is wearing *irkassène*, hide sandals tied on by cords of esparto grass which hold a piece of woollen stuff about the ankle. It is exactly like the simple sandals of the Greek and Roman shepherds.

Like the town-dwellers, the Berbers have numerous ways of wearing the burnous. This very simple garment thus acquires on them a variety of different appearances, with its side flaps thrown back over arms or shoulders, producing very beautiful effects of drapery.

The general appearance of this man from the Meknassa well illustrates the style of costume distributed throughout all the north-east, as far as the borders of Algeria.

His dress is lent its essential character by the very short *jellaba*, known as *ajejeb*. This is made of very dark brown, or sometimes black, wool with thin stripes, and it is also enriched with more or less lavish embroidery along the seams and coloured pompoms. In the past, it was worn with one arm passed out through the opening for the neck and was held in at the waist by means of a heavy leather belt decorated with brightly coloured patterns, the *darouet*. A magnificent leather satchel, *azaïbour*, tooled and embroidered, and decorated with long hanging thongs, was the pride of the countrymen of the Rif. Today, the *darouet* is scarcely ever worn and the *azaïbour* has finally been abandoned. The main reason for relinquishing these elements of traditional dress can be traced to sojourns in Algeria, where the Riffians go as seasonal labourers. People made fun of the satchels with their lengthy thongs and the mountain people of the Rif, being very sensitive to mockery, would sometimes go so far as to cut the thongs off their traditional *azaïbour*.

The peasant in Plate 18 is wearing the sandals called *disira nourouari* made of plaited esparto grass; when walking far a spare pair would be carried slung from the shoulder. The shirt, *achabir*, is of the standard pattern with wide sleeves. In the past, the headdress consisted of a simple camel-hair cord, *fourou*, wound several times round the head. Today, the white *rezza* is much more common and is increasingly coming into use throughout the Moroccan countryside.

Out of the house, the Riffian always carries his oaken staff, *adqabout*, from which he is inseparable.

(See details of the satchels in the appended pages of sketches.)

THE MOUNTAIN TRIBES OF CENTRAL MOROCCO

The Aït Oumalou

Already in the XIIth century of the Christian era, the Arab geographer al-Idrisi tells of the existence of two groups of Berber tribal confederations, whose territories were determined by the two faces of the Atlas mountains. The Aït Oumalou (the Sons of the Shaded Slope) lived on the north side of the mountainous chain; while the Beraber occupied the southern slopes of the Atlas and their lands extended as far as the valleys on the fringes of the Sahara.

The names for these groups are based on oral tradition. Nevertheless, it should be mentioned that throughout the area certain tribes from one group or the other are to be found embedded in the other's territory in a way which makes it impossible to set any very precise geographical limits between them.

During the course of history, the mountain tribes, like those in the fringe Saharan regions, have frequently fought among themselves over the possession of land, but equally have been intermittently in opposition to the central government, whenever it lacked the means to impose its authority. As a result, the territory occupied by the tribes refusing to submit to the central authority was called *«bled ciba»*, that is to say the «land of dissent».

The Aït Oumalou came into existence in a rugged heavily-forested area, which is very hard to penetrate. The harshness of the climate and the difficulties of everyday life gave them iron wills and, in the case of the men, an exceptional capacity for endurance. The Aït Oumalou were reputed to be invincible. Their ardour in battle and contempt of danger placed them in the foremost rank of the warrior peoples of North Africa.

From the plateaux of the Middle Atlas, the Aït Oumalou could reach the fertile plains of the north and the Berber dynasties were frequently compelled to fight them in order to contain them in their mountains.

Their geographical isolation, as well as their characters, kept them apart from external influences so that, from an ethnographic point of view, they constituted a real reservoir of traditions. I had the feeling that I was confronting individuals who had not changed their way of life for centuries.

Today, many of the Aït Oumalou are sedentary. But in the regions rich in pasture, the tribes still live in their tents and move with the seasons: in summer to the high mountains, in the winter to the plateaux or the plains, taking with them, in the unchanging cycle of transhumance, the vast herds which represent their principal wealth.

While the men keep watch, the women care for the animals, pitch or strike the tents and superintend their transportation. The migrations of this pastoral people present a spectacle which is both Biblical and picturesque.

At the head and on the flanks rides a wall of horsemen acting as sentinels, then the oxen, mules and mares heavily laden with black tents, various utensils, carpets, chickens hanging in bunches tied by their legs... The women dressed in white, their shoulders covered by a rectangular piece of woollen cloth, their legs sheathed in many coloured stockings, their heads bound in kerchiefs, black, orange or red, sometimes carrying a child on their backs, guide the progress of the convoy, helping up a fallen animal, rearranging a load, adjusting a packsaddle that is slipping. Next, with their shepherds, come the flocks of sheep and goats, a torrent which streams past with a noise of trampling hooves that drowns out all other sounds. Lastly, at the end of the procession, come more horsemen.

Pasture is the thing that is most important to these transhumants. They camp where grass is plentiful and leave as soon as it becomes scarce. If there is a lack of pasture-land, the herds die and the tribe is reduced to poverty.

The Aït Oumalou are not far-ranging nomads. The terrain is unsuited to it. All own some agricultural land and each clan has a *tirrhemt*, a fortified house where it can store its possessions.

The social organization is patriarchal. The head of the family is absolute master in his tent. He takes part in the tribal council and annually helps to elect the *cheikh el am* (leader for the year), generally in the spring. This leader is often no more than a puppet in the hands of some influential person of standing. But sometimes a man of greater stature imposes his authority in a more enduring way — for example, Moha ou Hammou of the Zaïan and Moha ou Saïd of the Aït Ouirrah some thirty years ago.

The Aït Oumalou are proud of being Muslim and many have a deep-seated veneration for their marabouts. Two families of saints have always exercised great influence over them, the Imhiouach and the Ihansalen, whose *zaouïa* was founded in the last years of the XIIth century.

Today, the Aït Oumalou live in peace and security, and devote themselves for the most part to increasing their livestock.

They remain faithful, however, to their ancient customs and in the evenings they gather in the glow of the camp fires to dance and sing, as their ancestors did before them, ancient songs of love and war. This is the *haïdous*, whose exact form varies from tribe to tribe. Most commonly the women stand in a long line, shoulder to shoulder, singing hour after hour and clapping their hands, while the men beat out the rhythm on their tambourines.

WOMAN OF THE AÏT MGUILD PLATE 19

The tribe of the Aït Mguild, settled on the slopes of the Middle Atlas, is made up of numerous sub-groups but nevertheless forms a very homogeneous unit and from the Irklaouène of Azrou to the Aït Messaoud in the higher regions, there is very little variation in dress.

This woman from the village of Aïn Leuh, of the Aït Mouli sub-group, represents the classical type of Aït Mguild Berber dressed to go to the market *(souk)*.

She is wearing the *izar*, the long piece of cloth in which every Berber woman covers her body. The size and material of the cloth may vary, as well as the way in which it is draped but in every country district one comes upon this form of clothing which owes something to both the Greek chiton and to the Roman peplum and represents the survival of a tradition, many thousands of years old, from the ancient peoples of the Mediterranean.

Berber women are marvellous weavers, but do not know how to sew and it is fair to say that nothing they wear is sewn, all is draped.

The cotton *izar* measures roughly 4.50 metres by 1.40 metres and envelops the body. It is held at the waist by a belt, *taggoust*, and in front of the shoulders by two silver fibulae, *tisernas*. These two pieces of jewellery are here hidden by the cloak, but the silver chain which links them can be seen. The cloak, called *hendira* in Arabic and *tamizart* in the *Tamazirht* dialects of Berber, is simply a small blanket of woollen cloth, woven by the women, and is a basic element in Berber dress. It is worn in various ways, thrown over the shoulders, tied under the chin by means of two cords, brought forwards over the head, etc. It is a very functional garment well suited to the plateaux of the Atlas which are, as has been so rightly said, «a cold land where the sun is hot». One does in fact find this traditional blanket in all the high altitude regions where, during the course of the same day, it may be necessary to face the rigours of a cold wind and the heat of a burning sun.

Of particular interest in the Berber regions are the patterns decorating this woollen *tamizart*, which vary from tribe to tribe. They serve to mark the tribal identity.

The *tamizart* of the Aït Mguild is striped with seven transversal rows of small geometric patterns. It is worn with these facing inwards, the outside being decorated with fringes and shining sequins. The woollen leggings, *tarriwin*, are the work of the men, who knit as they watch their herds. The leather sandals have high backs to the heels; they are called *taberbacht* (the many hued ones), on account of the patches of brilliantly coloured cloth with which they are decorated.

A headscarf, *takenboucht*, envelops the two intertwined plaits, the weight of which makes them droop a little on to the nape of the neck. It is held in place either by a headband or by a cord, *khit*, but always in such a manner as to form a kind of peak above the eyes.

(For the various stages of draping the *izar*, see the appended pages of sketches.)

The Aït Mguild woman of Plate 19 gives a good impression of a Berber woman in her everyday dress, whereas this woman of the neighbouring Zaïan tribe is here dressed for a special occasion. Her *izar* is worn longer and is of muslin with wide sleeves, also of muslin, resembling the *dfina* of the towns which is known as *farajiya* or *mansouria*. All these light cottons and more or less decorated muslins are imported. They are bought in the *souks* of the neighbouring towns and introduce the luxury of the city to the countryside, where they are gradually replacing simple cottons, now reserved for everyday wear.

Here, the *izar* is held in at the waist by means of a belt of stiff old-style brocade, *tabeqqast*, and also visible are the *tisernas*, the fibulae which pin the drapery together in front of the shoulders. These latter are of silver as, in principle, is all Berber jewellery, but those of the Zaïan are finely worked and are embellished with coloured enamels in which blue predominates. The *tisernas* are adorned with pretty pendants, *lanibrat*. The bracelets are *nnbaïl* (hinged) and *dbalij*. Large numbers of rings, *takhatène*, are worn by the Zaïan, as throughout the Middle Atlas. The large diadem which crowns the head, the *tasfift*, is set on top of a very wide turbanned headdress, *abougs*, especially made to receive it. It is composed of silver coins, *hassani*, and again shows evidence of a certain loss of tradition. For, in the past, all the jewels were made up from plaques of silver worked according to local taste, but today it is frequently found more convenient to make up the headdress from coins.

This Berber woman of the Zaïan is wearing a *tamizart* very similar to that of the Aït Mguild, but longer. Thrown slightly back on the shoulders, it allows a glimpse of the woven decoration on the inner surface. She wears *taberbacht* on her feet. The peasant women of this tribe, whose *izar* is usually shorter than the one shown here,

155

wear knitted leggings called *taferriwin*, like their neighbours, the Aït Mguild. These are in fact worn by most of the mountain tribes of the Middle Atlas.

This woman is lavishly tattooed on her hands, arms and neck, according to the local tradition *(caïda)*.

She is portrayed here in a posture taken from the *ahidous*, a type of singing in which the rhythm is reinforced by means of gestures and by the clapping of hands and which is accompanied by tambourines played by their male companions. It is a form of entertainment given at feasts or performed in honour of an important guest visiting the tribe.

(See details of the jewellery of the Middle Atlas in the appended pages of drawings.)

This Berber woman of the Zemmour is not wearing the *tamizart*, which makes it easier to see how the *izar* is draped — the technique is roughly the same throughout the Middle Atlas. The only variation is in the length to which the garment reaches down as well as in the form of the belt which holds it in at the waist. In this plate, it is possible to see exactly how the silver fibulae, *tisernas*, pin the *izar* together over the breast. They are exactly like the fibulae used in antiquity by the Greek and Roman women. It may very well be that this was the first item of jewellery known to womankind. Originally, it was a simple thorn, later becoming a metal pin which, in the course of time, became the object of a wide range of experiments in decoration. The ring added to the pin to form a fibula completed this useful jewel, making an extremely practical system of fastening which has been employed at all periods and in all regions. The use of the fibula is general throughout Morocco; there are many kinds of very different pattern, from the simplest to the most delicate, enhanced with rich decoration. Several typical examples can be seen in the appended plates.

The belt of the woman of the Zemmour is the luxurious *taggoust*, an enormous woollen girdle embellished with silver duros and shells, and wound three or four times round the body. It is further decorated with numerous little pompoms falling in bunches.

The head is covered by the *tasebnit*, which is bound round with a sort of turban made of several fancy tasselled cords, *khiout* (sing.: *khit*), decorated into sparkling sequins.

This woman's dress is really the costume for a fine day when the woollen *tamizart* is unneccessary and can be replaced by a simple square of white cotton. The *tamizart* of the Zemmour is one of the finest pieces of Berber weaving. It is decorated with a large number of small geometric motifs arranged in stripes in which red predominates on a white ground.

The tattoos of the Zemmour are meticulously and skilfully done and are easily recognized by their regularity. They rise in carefully drawn tiers up the lower part of the leg and the forearm. Let me here state, once and for all, as regards tattoos, that they are particularly prized in the Middle Atlas and in eastern Morocco, but are scarce in the Atlas and very rare in the Anti-Atlas and the villages of the Sahara. Originally tribal markings, they have increasingly become no more than bodily decorations and it is not uncommon to find an *ouchama* (tattooer), famous for her pretty designs, summoned from one tribe to another to practise her art.

Certain tattooed designs do sometimes, however, have either prophylactic or healing properties. They are then done when the child is very young: for example the little line on the nose prevents infantile diarrhoea, while another pattern on the cheek cures coughing.

Here we have a mountain woman of the Aït Serrhouchène, of the Aït Bouchaouène sub-group. The general appearance is more rustic and this effect is further accentuated by the rather coarse tattoos on the face.

The hairstyle merits attention. Two rolls of hair frame the face, confined at the ends by little cords of black wool, extraordinarily reminiscent of certain Chinese effects.

The *izar* is made of a light imported cotton much used throughout eastern Morocco. The kerchief consists of a large black scarf with white spots, which is replacing the older *toukaït*, a scarf which used to be woven in the tribe and has now become very rare. The enormous belt, the *tahezzamt*, is made of a great number of interlaced woollen cords in many colours. A square of crimson wool, *ketafia*, attached to the fibulae, *iserlaï*, covers the shoulders and hangs down at the back.

Here, the jewellery has a particularly local flavour. The *tassedit* (the necklace which covers the breast) and the *taounza*, a large head-ornament with pendants, are made up from sets of silver plates which are decorated with repoussé and niello work and joined together with little silver chains. The bracelets, *tanbalin* (sing.: *tanbalt*), complete this very homogeneous set of jewels, with its simple and characteristic geometric decoration. It is the expression of a folk traditon which in the past existed in every tribe, in very varied forms, before the taste for headdresses made of silver coins evolved, along with the general deterioration in the traditional crafts.

Among the Aït Jellidasen, a tribe of the important confederation of the Aït Ouarrain, traditions seem to have been better preserved. The region is hard to reach and is thus less liable to penetration by outside influences.

This Berber woman of the Aït Bahr sub-group is wearing the classic woollen blanket locally known as *taberdouat*. Here one of the practical uses of the garment is shown: folded back up like this on the back, the blanket can be used to carry all sorts of loads: the washing, fodder for the animals and also, often, a small child. Instead of being worn over the shoulders, in Aït Ouarrain country the *taberdouat* is attached under the arms by two decorative cords acting as shoulder straps.

During the winter, the women drape themselves in a blanket of very thick wool, *aaban*, which they weave themselves. In summer this is replaced by the *izar* shown here.

A scarf bound round the hair is in turn covered by a thick piece of woollen cloth, the *lhaf*. The earrings are *tikharziyin*. This Berber woman's ankles are adorned with silver rings, *ikhelkhalène* (sing.: *khelkhal*), jewels much worn by the women of the Middle Atlas and more especially by those of eastern Morocco.

Among the Aït Jellidasen, tattoos have very clearly preserved their character of clan markings and in this tribe, which is highly fragmented, a person in the know can easily recognize to which sub-group a woman belongs by her tattoos.

We have now examined in succession five types of costume worn by the mountain women of central Morocco. They give a representative idea of the general character of the clothing in use among the numerous tribes, ranging from the Zemmour in the west to the Aït Ouarrain in the east. It will have been observed that the differences extend to all the elements, from the headdress to the jewellery, the belts, the methods of draping and in particular to the patterns which the women weave into their woollen cloak, which is called *hendira*, *tamizart* or *taberdouat*, depending on the region. Its decoration is a very important guide since it makes it possible to tell at a glance to which tribe — and even sub-group of the tribe — the woman wearing it belongs.

(For details of sandals from the Middle Atlas, see the appended pages of sketches.)

Male dress throughout the Middle Atlas shows no very remarkable characteristics. More or less everywhere, it consists of the *jellaba* and the *burnous*, this latter called *aselham* or *khaddoun* when it is of white wool and *khaïdous* or *azennar* when it is of goat or camel hair, worn with a shirt and trousers. The rustic mountain *jellaba* is called *tajellabit*; the woollen *haïk* is also frequently worn.

In the larger villages, leather sandals called *blari* (a pair: *belra*) are worn as in the towns, but the peasantry in the mountains wear esparto grass sandals, *tioulaï*, or sandals of dried hide, *tisila ourous*.

The head often quite simply has a camelhair cord wrapped around it a few times, leaving the shaved skull bare. The *rezza* or *chedd* is also worn, in the form of a more or less voluminous turban, on which a wide hat of reed or of esparto grass is perched in summer. That of the Zemmour, worn by the Berber in Plate 24, is well known for its huge size and wealth of decoration. It is, indeed, enriched by lavish woollen embroideries and numerous multicoloured pompoms. It is called *taraza*, or again *chemrourou* (from Spanish *sombrero*). The man shown here is wearing the classic Zemmour dress for taking part in the famous horse races of Khemisset which, on the occasion of certain great feasts, pit the finest horsemen of the tribe against each other.

A curious garment worn by the mountain people of the Aït Oumalou of the High Atlas is the *tabbane*. It is a kind of long thick pair of drawers knitted in natural wool and striped brown and white.

This garment is very useful as a protection against the rigours of the winter at high altitude and is put on when the cold weather arrives and not removed again until the fine weather returns. A little opening is made in it to serve as a fly.

The *tabbane* is worn in particular by hunters and it is said that it makes it possible for the Berbers when hunting the wild Barbary sheep to spend hours on the watch with snow up to their waists.

This piece of clothing is certainly of very ancient origin and it is interesting to note that it is represented in the paintings on certain Etruscan vases. This garment, not very widely used, is worn by the Berbers of the Ouanergui, the Aït Bou Gemmez and the Aït Bou Oulli.

The Beraber

Unlike the Aït Oumalou (the Sons of the Shaded Slope), the Beraber occupy the south-facing lands. They inhabit a large part of the Moroccan south-east, from the Atlas Mountains to the Sahara and from the River Dra to the borders of Algeria.

They are divided into two great confederations: the Aït Atta of the Sahara and the Aït Yafelman.

At the time when I undertook my study, the composition of these groups appeared as follows:

on the one hand, the Aït Atta were divided into five *khoms*, these in turn split into scattered tribes (Aït Yazza, Aït Ounebgui, Aït Ouallal, Aït Ouahlim, Aït Ounir);

on the other, the Aït Yafelman, were made up of the Aït Morrhad, Aït Hadiddou, Aït Izdeg, Aït Yahia, Aït Ayyach and the Aït Ouafellah.

They all proudly call themselves *«imazirhen»*, which means «free men» and they are all proud of their race. After epic battles, these two great groups have reached a state of balance with the following geographical distribution: the Aït Yafelman firmly hold the peaks of the Atlas and their southern slopes as far as the talweg of the Todrha and of the Rheris; the Aït Atta occupy the heights of the Anti-Atlas and the lands on the fringes of the Sahara between the Dra and the Tafilelt.

The Aït Atta and the Aït Yafelman are essentially shepherds, moving their flocks seasonally between mountain and lowland pastures. Many of them prefer the tent to the houses of the settled peoples, because it is, for them, a sign of nobility. Many consider the cultivation of the soil to be a mark of debasement and leave the care of the palm trees and of those few crops which are made possible by irrigation to the Quebala. We will mention these latter again in the chapter on the sedentary peoples of the oases of the south.

Among the Beraber tribes of the Atlas, certain elements of clothing found among the peoples of the Middle Atlas reappear.

WOMAN OF THE AÏT IZDEG
PLATE 26

This woman of the Aït Izdeg from the Midelt region is wearing an *izar* which reaches down very low. It is made of an imported brocaded cotton. The upper part hangs down far enough to hide the belt, *afkas*, which can scarcely be seen.

The long white *tamizart* is decorated with very simple black stripes, each with a narrow orange central stripe. The head, wrapped in several scarves, is covered by the *tassebnit* — a square of brilliantly coloured silk. The headdress is completed by a thick decorative cord, *khit*, which forms a bulky turban of dark purplish red hue, a colour particularly liked by the Aït Izdeg.

Here, the whole set of jewellery is made up from silver coins and it may be compared with that worn by the woman of the Aït Serrouchène in Plate 22, who is wearing jewellery whose elements are combined together in a very similar way, but are of ancient manufacture. Apart from the fibulae, *tisernas*, these are the necklaces, *tazra-n-ihorrin takhatart* (large) and *tamezziant* (small), the pectoral *tazra-n-chaït*, the necklace of gold louis, urban in origin, *methoua*, and the little necklace of glittering glass beads, *gadinaro*, a recently introduced item of costume jewellery.

Among the tattoos, those on the nose are peculiar to the women of the Aït Izdeg, who also rouge their cheeks lavishly with the red colouring, *aker*.

In the Atlas mountains, because of the rigorous nature of the winters at high altitude, the women weave thick *hiyak* of wool which they wear during the period of greatest cold. That of the Aït Hadiddou, the *tachkount*, is remarkable for the quality of its decoration. This long piece of woollen cloth has across its width two broad purplish-red stripes, which, when the *haïk* is draped, follow the vertical line of the wearer's body. Large numbers of strands of wool are left protruding at each side.

WOMAN OF THE AÏT HADIDDOU
PLATE 27

The bulk of the hair, tightly plaited on top of the head, is bound closely in place with a black handkerchief and the headdress, *aquellouz*, assumes the form of the crest of a helmet. Hide sandals, *irkassen*, protect the feet.

The women of the Aït Hadiddou also use the *tamizart* — theirs has narrow stripes of black, white and blue — which they wear on less cold days.

The Aït Morrhad, neighbours of the Aït Hadiddou, live on the southern slopes of the Atlas, their territory reaching down as far as Goulmima. The method of draping used by the women of this tribe is among the most beautiful in Morocco. The *izar*, which may be of white or blue cotton, reaches down to the feet and the women arrange its folds with an instinctive sense of the noble which is truly admirable. The woollen cloak called *tabizart* again forms part of the costume.

WOMAN OF THE AÏT MORRHAD
PLATE 28

The hairstyle of the Aït Morrhad is very remarkable. It is determined by rigorously fixed custom *(caïda)* and the two enormous plaits which are turned back

159

upwards to frame the face with absolute symmetry give the wearer a somewhat Egyptian look. A small chain, *assensir*, attached by a hook, normally crowns the summit. On important feast-days she may also wear the two silver ornaments which are here seen adorning her headdress: these are the *touaba*, convex silver disks with pendants.

This Berber woman is wearing around her neck the great necklace of amber, *loubane*, which is to be found, with variants, all over the south. The women of the Aït Morrhad also very often wear a small necklace composed of a row of baroque pearls or glass beads, *taratza*.

WOMAN OF THE AÏT
ATTA OF THE RETEB
PLATE 29

The sub-group of the Aït Atta to which this woman belongs is typical of a section of the Aït Atta of the Sahara who have settled in a fertile region, the Reteb, on the banks of the river Ziz.

This Berber woman of the Aït Atta is one of those southerners commonly called «blue women» because of the *izar* in which they drape themselves. This is made from a material called *khent*, a type of cotton cloth which used in the past to come from Guinea. It is dyed with indigo and the colour comes off, giving the skin a bluish tinge which appeals to the women of the south. *Khent* is in general use throughout the south of Morocco beyond the Atlas mountains. It should be mentioned, however, that as everywhere else, white remains the rule for feast days.

The upper and the lower edges of the *tamizart* are striped in white, black and red and are decorated by large numbers of woollen pompoms. The hairstyle is very special: thick plaits are held in a ring by a circle of leather and wool which acts as a support for the entire structure of hair. The whole is covered by a red *tassebnit*, and one or two coloured cords enhance the overall effect and hang down the nape of the neck.

The great necklace of amber, *loubane*, sits as it were on the shoulders and is secured rather low behind to counterbalance it. One can make out the fibulae with pendants attached, *tisernas amriya*, joined by a silver chain. This Berber woman's wrists are adorned with the ancient spiked bracelets, *izebgan*, typical of the south. In the past, these were valuable as defensive weapons, in addition to their charm as jewellery. They were valuable to the women who, during raids *(razzias)*, used to inflict severe blows with them on their attackers when it came to hand-to-hand fighting.

In this tribe, there is another piece of clothing not shown in the plate — the blue veil, *khenita*. It is, as its name suggests, a rectangle of *khent* about two metres long, in which the women wrap themselves out-of-doors so that even their faces are completely covered. The weave of the cloth is open enough for them to be able to see through it sufficiently to walk about and it is in this excessively coy dress that the women of the Aït Atta of the Reteb leave their homes or appear before strangers.

(For the draping of the *khenita*, see the appended pages of drawings.)

WOMAN OF THE
MSOUFFA
PLATE 30

The *gna*, the veil worn by this woman of the Msouffa, is reminiscent of the *litham* of the Almoravids, the first Moroccan dynasty of Berber origin, which came up out of the Western Sahara and to whom we owe the founding of the city of Marrakesh. The Msouffa of the Fezouata in the valley of the Dra are in fact their direct descendants.

The *gna* is cut from very fine and slightly glazed cotton, purplish in colour, called *kalamoun*.

MAN OF THE AÏT
KHALIFA
PLATE 31

Among the men's costumes of the Beraber, that of the Aït Khalifa is of particular interest.

The Aït Khalifa, who are nomads roaming the Tafilelt region to the east of the

160

Oued Ziz, generally have a proud bearing. Over his long tunic and white *burnous*, *aselham*, this man is wearing the short-sleeved striped *jellaba* of the south, called *tajellabit*.

This *tajellabit* is always recognizable by the patterns woven into it, but the shape too is special: it is split up the front like a *burnous*, which makes it possible to throw the side flaps back over the shoulders without putting the arms in the sleeves, for ease of movement.

On his feet he is wearing the classic *naïl* worn by all the nomads of the Sahara. These are simple leather soles held in place by a cord of esparto grass which passes between the big and second toes and ties at the ankle. The head is wrapped in the *chèche*, a long white scarf, which protects the face and neck from the burning sand.

Those Beraber who do not wear the *tajellabit* dress in a shirt, a *burnous* and, at high altitudes, a *jellaba* of coarse wool and sometimes also a *haïk* draped as we have seen on the man from the Chaouïa in Plate 16. In the south, men do not always wear the *seroual* and, during fine weather, the shirt is often their only piece of clothing. It is open on the shoulder, being closed by two cords at the neck, and only the cut of the wide sleeves may vary a little from one region to another. Its shape and general appearance can be seen in Plate 39, which portrays an inhabitant of the Dra valley.

THE SEDENTARY PEOPLES
OF THE SOUTHERN OASES

The oases of southern Morocco, strung out along the valleys of the Guir, the Ziz, the Rheris, the Todrha, the Dadès and the Dra, form little islands of greenery at each break in the Bani range and are inhabited by sedentary peoples known, depending on the region, as Draoua, Regaga, Filala or Quebala. This last term means «man of the south» and is generic in character.

These sedentary peoples are divided into two quite distinct groups on the basis of their origins: the *harrar* (the literal translation of which is free, genuine man) and the *harratine*. The former are racially white, Arab or Berber, and came to the country either as warriors, or as exiles fleeing their tribe of origin. They then allied themselves with other whites descended from ancient independent tribes which had been broken up by the perpetual warring, and with them formed new social groupings. Incapable of any real cohesion because of their disparate origins, the *harrar* were at the mercy of the solidly established tribes and live the same life as the *harratine*.

These latter are black, or the result of a mixing of white and black. Most of them are descendants of slaves imported in the past from Senegal or the Sudan by traders who had regular commercial relations with the market at Timbuktu. Some of them would also appear to be the last descendants of the ancient black race indigenous to Africa which, according to certain classical authors, was still living along the southern and northern edges of the Sahara at the beginning of the Christian era.

Here, I would like to state my personal opinion as an artist who visited these groups of people and lived among them while carrying out my studies. All along the chain of oases on the fringes of the Sahara, I came across small groups which one may truly regard as surviving islands of a very ancient race. They are quite different in appearance from the other Quebala — their physical type in fact suggests that of the so-called «Ethiopians» of antiquity and their copper skin could not possibly be confused with that of the other negroid elements in the population.

Today, all the Quebala, no matter what their colour or race, live together in *ksour* (sing.: *ksar*), great fortified villages built of rammed earth and with flat roofs. These constructions are often vast — the architecture is almost always massive, yet well-balanced. They often give an impression of elegance and this serves to further underline the grace and harmony of their decoration.

These villages are little cities in which the social life and each individual's obligations are perfectly defined and regulated. They are often administered by a *djemaa*, that is to say a council of notables, which is frequently assisted by another council composed of representatives elected annually, or at regular intervals, by all the heads of families.

The *harrar* usually control the local life, but occasionally it is the *harratine* who are in charge of the affairs of the community.

163

The Quebala are farmers. They tend the palms, cultivate the land and, by what seems a miracle, maintain marvellous orchards. And since in this arid land nothing can be done without water, necessity has made them masters in the difficult art of irrigation. Their efforts must undoubtedly appear rudimentary to hydraulic technicians but, nevertheless, the Quebala are unparalleled in their ability to tap the water of a spring and lead it, often for a very great distance, either on the surface or by way of underground channels, to the plot of land they plan to cultivate. With no instruments of any kind and no formal calculations, they carefully choose the most economic gradient. Here empiricism and intuition take the place of science.

But these peaceful farmers are not warriors. They have never been able to defend the oases, the fruit of their toil, against the greed of the Arab, and in particular of the Berber, nomads. In order to avoid pillage and depredation, they have thus been forced to place themselves under the protection of these same nomads and to pay them annual tribute.

The Beraber, who consider working the soil to be beneath them, have made a speciality of this form of «protection» and it was frequent in the past for a sub-group of the Aït Atta to take up arms against another sub-group of the same confederation in order to avenge an injury done to one of its tributaries.

This system resulted in a great deal of abuse. It could hardly be otherwise. But all in all, it made it possible for the sedentary peoples to cultivate their palm groves, for the nomads understood perfectly, as one of their leaders so neatly put it, that «the herdsman who kills his milch-cow through ill-treatment is pretty stupid.»

The life of the sedentary peoples of the oases of the south is a constant fight against a hostile nature. If there is a shortage of water or if the wadi dries up, famine makes its appearance with its trail of disease and misfortune. Therefore, when evening comes, the Quebala love to gather merrily in order to forget the toils of the day and the trials of the morrow.

At the foot of the high walls of the *ksar*, the women dressed in their most beautiful clothes and adorned with heavy jewels, line up side by side, while the men squat and beat out on their frame-drums the rhythms of their companions' songs and dances. As the darkness gathers, great fires of palm fronds are lit which illuminate the scene with a lurid glow and the *ahouach*, as this typically Berber celebration is called, continues far into the night.

WOMAN OF THE AHEL
TODRHA
PLATE 32

Throughout the Moroccan south, blue *khent* is the material preferred by the women, but there are a few exceptions to this general rule: the women of the Ahel Todrha (the People of Todrha), for example, are dressed differently. They drape an *izar* of white cotton in a very special way over a black *toubit*. The *izar* is worn so that it, as it were, crosses over diagonally from both sides and is knotted on each shoulder. It is not held in by belt and the ends float free at the sides.

The headscarf, which is always black, encloses two plaits coiled at the nape of the neck. The make-up is curious: a large area under each eye is blackened with *harquous* and the face is striped vertically with red lines of *aker*.

The size of the bracelets is noteworthy. They are made of solid silver and are the heaviest I ever came across in Morocco. They sometimes weigh more than a pound and, as the women wear two on each wrist, they have to place a round piece of leather, held in place with pitch, between them to avoid having their skin pinched and bruised.

(For the various stages of cross-draping the *izar*, see the appended pages of drawings.)

Just as the people of the oases of the Todrha bear the name of Ahel Todrha, so do those who live in the *ksour* of the Dadès valley take that of Ahel Dadès (the People of the Dadès). Arbitrary but convenient, these names are used to designate the whole complex of splintered and confused ethnic groups which make up the population of these fringe Saharan villages.

The influence of the Aït Atta is very strong in the Middle Dadès and many women there have adopted the manner of the Berbers of that tribe in the draping of their robe. The *izar* is of *khent* and the blue veil is arranged over a high semi-circle of wool and leather fixed firmly to the head, which gives the hairstyle the shape of a halo.

The general effect of these draperies is one of quiet distinction, which brings to mind the noblest pictures from the Bible.

The woman of the Imerrhane in Plate 34 is representative of those found slightly to the north of the Dadès valley, at the level of Skoura. She is dressed for a festival, that is to say wearing an *izar* in white cotton. It is draped over a coloured *toubit*, crossed on the breast and at the back, according to a particular tradition *(caïda)* which, it must be added, extends from the Dadès to part of the Atlas and Anti-Atlas. The Berber women of the Glaoua even go so far as to cross the *izar* almost in the centre of the breast. The fibulae which hold it in place may actually be touching and the flap of drapery which hangs down at the back from the shoulders looks like a little cloak.

The headdress of the Imerrhane is highly individual: two long plaits, each ending in a silver coin, fall on either side of the face, while two other plaits mixed with wool hang down behind the ears, wrapped in a scarf of dark red wool. On top of this can be seen the head ornament called *talgamout* (the small bit). It consists of a frontal element decorated with cloisonné enamels and held in place by little silver chains which run back over the head. It is held at the back by a hook. This head ornament is also very widespread among the Glaoua and in the Anti-Atlas, where it exists in a variety of forms. Around Skoura, a diadem of silver coins and coral beads, *sfifa*, is often worn with it.

The Mesguita are Draoua, Quebala whose ethnic characteristics have been described already.

As always, the everyday clothing is of *khent*, but the woman shown here is dressed for a special occasion. She is, furthermore, the wife of a great chief, which explains the presence of gold jewellery among her ornaments. As a general rule, the jewellery in the countryside is of silver, but it is interesting to note that when a rich caïd from the Atlas or the south wants to show off his wealth, he buys gold jewellery in the town to adorn the women of his harem, in this way introducing into his household something of the urban luxury so admired by country folk. Here, the *taba*, the fibulae pinning the *izar*, the buckle of the belt and the earrings are all of gold and of urban origin. The tiara, *tasfift*, on the other hand, is very much a local form of headdress; it is covered with small pearls and decorated with antique gold coins, *hassani*. The hairstyle is very original: the hair is divided into two braided wings which finish as rounded plaits on either side of the face. These plaits end in silver decorations, *azizat*, to which antique Berber pendants in filigree silver, called *tishgagalin*, are attached.

Here, now, is the representation of a woman from the Dra, wearing the everyday *izar* of blue *khent*. She is carrying a heavy earthenware pitcher, *goula*, in the small of her back, as is the local custom. An ingenious little padded cushion softens the impact of the hard jar on the spinal column.

This woman is from a group of *harratine* living on the banks of the Dra betwee Adgz and Rebat of the Tinzouline. The *hartaniat* are often extremely attractive They apparently expend all their coquetry in inventing original hairstyles, whic vary from oasis to oasis.

The hairstyle of the *hartaniat* of the Upper Dra is very remarkable — a exaggeration of that of the women of the Mesguita. The way in which it is achieve is wonderfully systematic: two thick plaits descend in graceful and rigorousl symmetrical curves ending, at the breast, in two large ornaments, *tassta*, made c small silver coins and coral beads arranged alternately. The lower part of each pla is encircled by rings of silver, *tassassout*, and of amber, *talakhirt.* The headdres enhanced by a small diadem of coins and coral, *agoued*, is also embellished wit amulets, *tabouert*, and small ornaments of silver and shells, *tibouahin.* The earring *tikhorsin*, are decorated in their centres with *rjel el hamman* (pigeon's feet).

The *hartaniat* are not tattooed. They say that the blue of the tattoos would n show up against the deep colour of their skin. Those of the Dra replace this kin of bodily decoration by numerous painted designs on the face. The patterns, whic are sometimes very delicate and elaborate, have nothing to do with personal tast and for great occasions all the women of the same group of *harratine* will have the faces embellished with the same decorative motifs.

There is a very wide range of these motifs and they vary from group to grou all along the Dra valley. They are painted in black (with *harquous*), red (with *ake* and orange (with *zafran*), in such a way that they will last for several weeks.

(See details of the jewels from the southern oases in the appended pages c sketches.)

The hairstyle of the *hartaniat* from the Ziz valley is one of the most remarkabl of the Moroccan south. The hair is divided in the middle and numerous small plai support two other enormous ones, the *dmouj* (horns), which extend right round to th back of the head and then fall as far as the waist, lengthened by two woollen tassel *ifili n-wachioune.* A decoration made of small overlapping silver roundels, *doual* descends in the form of a ribbon down the central line between the plaits. A simila but smaller ornament, the *soualef*, is wrapped around the head. Numerous shel and coral beads, silver trinkets and amulets complete this skilful piece of hairdressin

The *hartaniat* of the Ziz wear the *ketafiya*, a square of red woollen cloth whic is attached in front of the fibulae which fasten the *izar* and hangs backwards ove the shoulders.

Plate 39 shows a Draoui from Ktaoua. This man is wearing a very ample tuni which in summer is usually the only piece of clothing worn by most of the peasan of the Moroccan south. This tunic is fastened on one shoulder at the neck by mear of a cord. The Draoui shown here is prepared to play at *takora* and is holding i his hand a curved stick made from a palm branch, *akouraï. Takora* is a game wit very ancient origins. It is well-known throughout North Africa and is very simila to hockey. The players are divided into two teams and, in order to score a poin they must hit a kind of chuck, *takourt*, behind the rear line of the opponents' sid Ancient magical rites are still associated with this game, which in former days wa played principally in times of drought with the aim of causing it to rain.

THE CHLEUH

The volcanic mountain mass of the Siroua and the western part of the Anti-Atlas between the Dra and the Atlantic are inhabited by sedentary Berbers, who refer to themselves by the general name of « Chleuh ».

The Chleuh have lived in this area since time immemorial. Industrious, abstemious and hard-working, they strive ceaselessly to develop an unproductive land to which they are passionately attached. They are extremely ingenious. Everywhere, on the hillsides, stretch level after level of terraces, carefully manured and watered by irrigation ditches, *séguia*, which follow the contours of the mountain, sometimes for very considerable distances, in order to bring water from the spring to the field that is to be rendered fertile.

Rainwater is collected in numerous cisterns, reserves which are jealously guarded until needed during the dry season.

In spite of this ingenuity and in spite of the ceaseless and exhausting toil, the land cannot feed all its children. The rocky nature of the ground and the precariousness of the water supply make it impossible to extend the cultivated area beyond the limits already reached by men centuries ago.

As a consequence the Chleuh are forced into self-exile in order to support their families remaining behind in the home country. Many are grocers in the northern towns and one can say that almost all the small-scale grocery businesses of Marrakesh, Mogador, Safi, Casablanca, Rabat and Tangiers are in their hands. Others, less lucky, are employed in humbler occupations.

Others again cross the seas and go to work in factories in France and other European countries. There, grouped in colonies from a single place of origin, they work hard to save money which is sent to their families who have stayed at home.

After a certain number of years, the exile returns home to his native village where he resumes his place and one of his relatives leaves in his turn in order to keep the family.

In the past, the Chleuh tribes were organized into little independent « republics » governed by a council of elders.

Sometimes these small states assumed the form of an oligarchy. Sometimes, after breaking the democratic framework, the personal power of a chief asserted itself.

The political life was intense. All these republics were divided into rival factions, each of which had its counterpart in the other tribes, like the Guelphs and Ghibelines of medieval Italy.

These struggles have ended, but the memory of them is very much alive and still, to a large extent, influences the present.

The Anti-Atlas is the chosen land of saints. Each tribe, each sub-group, each village has one or more sanctuaries where the mortal remains of some holy man are preserved. The Chleuh are indeed fervent Muslims. They are proud of having given North African Islam several of its most eminent mystical reformers, such as the Imam Jazouli of the Ida ou Semlal, who lived in the XVIth century and founded a religious order which played an important role even beyond the frontiers of Morocco.

Everywhere else, in the plains and even in the mountains of the Atlas and of the Rif, there are to be found numerous marabouts descended from a saint who came from the Chleuh country.

This religious fervour has encouraged the development of small maraboutic states in the Anti-Atlas. The best known is that of the marabouts of the Tazeroualt, founded in the XVIth century by Sidi Ahmed ou Moussa, the celebrated patron of the graceful acrobats and dancers who can be seen all over the country.

The Chleuh has a frank open nature. He is intelligent, intuitive and capable. He has an astonishing ability to assimilate and to adapt. Nevertheless, no matter how advanced he is, he remains attached to his age-old traditions and customs. Once back in his tribe, his world reclaims him and nothing marks him off from his brother who remained at home.

He is also a sharply satirical poet, quickwitted and full of irony. The professional poets and bards who go from tribe to tribe are always well received and the best of them are piously remembered.

The heart of the Anti-Atlas, peopled by tribes who for so long lived shut in upon themselves, is still the least-known part of Morocco. Everywhere, there are signs of a very rich local folk tradition, much better preserved than in the other regions.

The Ida ou Nadif live in the mountains to the south of the Wadi Souss at an altitude approaching 1,000 metres. In spite of the southerly latitude, the winters are harsh and thick woollen clothing is worn, similar to that of the mountain people of the Atlas.

The voluminous *haïk* worn by this young girl of the Ida ou Nadif is called *afaggou*. To my mind, this garment is one of the most beautiful pieces of weaving from the Berber country. It is roughly 4 metres by 1.30 metres. Its edges and corners are decorated with exquisitely executed motifs in various colours, woven in an infinite variety of geometric patterns, enhanced with delicate embroidery. The *afaggou* is held in at the waist by a huge woollen belt, the *tassmert*, which further accentuates the rather bunched up overall appearance.

The abundance of jewellery is very noticeable. This is so throughout the whole mountainous region of the Anti-Atlas, where fine quality ornaments are found generally known as jewels from the Souss.

The jewels of the Ida ou Nadif are of niello-worked silver, enhanced by cabochons of red glass imitating garnets. They are highly prized and are often worn in the neighbouring tribes. In this area, which is *tachelhaït* speaking, the fibulae are called *tizerzaï* and the small ornaments which form their connecting chain, *arouz*.

The hairstyle, *tizrourin*, is made up of numerous small plaits, three of which hang in front of each shoulder. The others fall down at the back onto the *akhazi*, a square of blue wool embroidered in brilliant colours, the two upper corners of which can be seen attached to the *tizerzaï*. The sumptuous locally-made *taounza* covers the head and its pendants reach down almost to in front of the eyes. The earrings are *tikhourzin ouguelnin*; around the neck, a necklace, *tifilit louban*, made of great spherical beads of amber, embellished with coloured stones and silver duros. The bracelets are not peculiar to the tribe; they are found throughout the Anti-Atlas.

The sandals, which are of a pattern worn throughout all the mountain tribes of the Anti-Atlas, are called *loqchini*. They are made of red leather, with very projecting soles and heels which reach halfway up the back of the calf.

(For details of the hairstyles of the Ida ou Nadif, see the appended pages of drawings).

We find again here, being worn by this woman of the Ida ou Kensous, a neighbouring tribe of the Ida ou Nadif, the *afaggou* already described, but with a veil covering the head. This latter is the *adrar*, a big square of white woollen cloth decorated with pompoms at the four corners. A black frontlet bound about her head holds it in place. This veil is worn exclusively by married women.

The jewels are the same as those we have seen in the preceding plate. The size of the earrings should be noted — a hook attached to the frontlet helps the earlobe to support the weight.

WOMAN OF THE IDA OU KENSOUS
PLATE 41

The Aït Abd Allah is a mountain tribe whose villages lie between 1,500 and 2,000 metres in altitude.

One does not usually imagine a Moroccan looking like the Berber woman in this plate, who in her overall appearance calls to mind rather an Eskimo. The thick *haïk* is of white wool, rather rough in texture and quite undecorated. The back panel has been brought up onto the shoulders. It is the way of wearing the *adrar* which gives the whole its very unexpected character. We still have the same square of wool covering the head, but here half of it has been dyed black and its big tassels, *tioutsatsin*, have been dipped in henna. The women often put these up on top of the head by knotting the four corners of the *adrar* together, to produce this picturesque headdress.

The sandals are again *loqchini*, the soles of which are square and very protruding.

WOMAN OF THE AÏT ABD ALLAH
PLATE 42

The southern slopes of the Anti-Atlas are furrowed by wadis, which flow towards the Dra valley. Sedentary peoples live along their banks, and the Issafène are established along the upper valley of the Wadi Akka.

When we leave the mountains behind, the usual garment once again becomes the blue *izar*. Among the Issafène, this is draped in such a way as to give the effect of a kind of dress, much pleated at the waist, and falling very low and very full.

Under her blue *izar*, this woman is wearing a *toubit*, the sleeves of which just show. This *toubit* may be of any colour, but it seems that pale blue, mauve and saffron yellow are preferred.

Here once again, we find the *tassmert*, the thick red and black belt common to many of the tribes of the Anti-Atlas and also the head veil with pompoms — but here it is of blue cotton, like the *izar*, and is called *tizakouin*. It is worn in various ways: it may simply fall over the head, covering it completely; it may also be worn with the pompoms drawn up and tied together as we saw in Plate 42. Here, only two of the pompoms have been raised and tied together, allowing a little of the hairstyle to show. This is called *taggourt* and, in accordance with the local custom, consists of some thirty little braids plaited very thinly and tightly and attached at the back to a band decorated with cowries, *tiroulalin*.

This woman of the Issafène is wearing the *akhasi* already mentioned in Plate 40. This garment is found fairly frequently throughout the whole of the south and was apparently designed to receive the plaits hanging down at the back. The red sandals with projecting soles and high backs are called *idoukan* (sing.: *adak*).

The jewels are very abundant and different from those of the neighbouring tribes to the north. They are closely related to those of the southern Anti-Atlas, where the tribe of the Ammeln seems to make a speciality of them. The *tizerzaï* preferred by the Issafène are triangular, heavily worked and delicately pierced, adorned with a large central cabochon. The chain which normally joins the two fibulae is here replaced by a complicated ornament, *issersel*, whose centre is decorated with an elongated ball of silver filigree brightened by enamels, the *taguemmout*, with its three pendants. In the middle of the big necklace may be observed an element which is very widespread in the Anti-Atlas, *lherz* (pl.: *lehrouz*).

WOMAN OF THE ISSAFÈNE
PLATE 43

Among the Issafène, the women wear a little head ornament which can be seen here, partly hidden by the veil: this is the *leftoul*, made of a couple of dozen large rings threaded on a plaited cord.

Of the bracelets which she is wearing the open one, *azbeg* (pl.: *ibezgan*) is a jewel typical of the Anti-Atlas.

The women of the Issafène are not tattooed. They barely touch up the red of their lips and cheeks with *aker*. On the other hand, they stain the upper part of their foreheads and all round the edges of their faces a yellow-orange colour by means of saffron. They also have the charming habit of slipping a little bunch of green leaves under their diadem, so that the colour contrasts pleasantly with that of the saffron.

WOMAN OF TAGMOUT
SINGING THE AHOUACH
PLATE 44

We have just seen a Berber woman of the Issafène with her *tizakouin* raised. Here now is a woman from Tagmout, with her face entirely veiled.

Tagmout is on the banks of the Wadi Tata, which runs parallel to the Wadi Akka. The women's clothes are broadly the same as those of the Issafène, but the veil, *tizakouin*, is replaced by the *aferoual* in black or blue with light fringes.

This woman of Tagmout is shown performing one of the movements of the *ahouach* which is, roughly speaking, for the people of the south what the *ahidous* is for those of the north.

In a group of women singing the *ahouach*, some have their faces uncovered. Those who are married and whose husbands are present, have their faces completely veiled with a piece of open weave blue cotton, as we see shown in this plate. On festival days, a scarf of striped red silk, *tassebnit*, is added to the *aferoual*.

This woman is wearing embroidered sandals, *rrihit*.

In addition to garments of blue cotton, those living in the southern valleys of the Anti-Atlas are familiar with the white *izar* and the woollen *afaggou*, the latter being worn much more rarely, on cold days.

The jewellery shows no important local variant forms. However young unmarried girls, in accordance with a local custom of Tagmout, wear, one on top of the other two small diadems, the *leftoul* and the *khouatem*, made of rings and other decorative objects threaded on a black braid.

WOMAN OF THE
AMMELN
PLATE 45

The valley of the Ammeln is in the heart of the Ida ou Semlal, a tribe whose jewellers are renowned for their great skill. All the tribes of the southern slopes of the Anti-Atlas buy jewellery from them. The jewels of the Ammeln women are very numerous and they wear them even with their everyday dress. Often they go out together to fetch fodder, which they carry on their backs in charming decorated baskets, *azgaou*, which are held in position by means of a thick cord which passes across their foreheads, like a yoke. Their enormous silver fibulae and voluminous necklaces shine against the dark blue of their clothing and provide a pretty decorative touch. But it is difficult, particularly for a man, to observe these charming ornaments as closely as might be wished, for the women of the Ammeln are extremely reserved, the most difficult to approach in Morocco. The Ammeln are, it should be added, devout Muslims, very strict in their principles, and it is said of this part of the country that it is the «Moroccan Mzab». The shyness of the women is such that I was never able, out-of-doors, to draw near a group of them without their immediately veiling their faces with a flap of their *izar* and fleeing like a flock of sparrows.

The woman in Plate 45 is covered in the jewels worn for a special occasion. The fibulae called *tikhoullalin* are very large, flat and thin, finely engraved and embellished with enamels. The *issersel* which joins them is decorated in the centre with a great silver ball, *taguemmout*, which can be attached to the *izar* by means of a hook.

The necklaces, *tifoulout loubane*, are enormous in size: between the usual great spherical amber beads are inserted little black stones with white spots, *lhabouben*, and long beads of coral, *merjane*. The diadem of amber and silver, *mechbouach*, is attached to the head covering, *tacheddat*, from which a fringe of hair is allowed to escape. The earrings, *imjeran*, are embellished with numerous little silver coins. The bracelets are of the usual type to be found more or less everywhere in the Anti-Atlas: they are an expression of the folk culture of the Ammeln. With a few rare exceptions, the jewellers here are Jewish, as throughout Morocco, and certain Jewish communities, of which the most important is that of Tahala, have made a speciality of producing jewellery. Their craftsmen sell their work outside the tribe, and sometimes, in order to practise their craft, even settle in the neighbouring tribes: in this way the designs they are in the habit of making have spread.

The way in which they operate commercially is as follows: when a Berber woman has saved up a certain sum, she places an order with a jeweller and provides him with his raw material in the form of silver coins, agreeing at the same time on the price of the workmanship. On the same principle, when a worn out piece of jewellery is sold it is valued in terms of its weight of silver, plus a little extra representing the cost of its manufacture, which is generally around a quarter of its value by weight. This is a common custom throughout the whole Berber area. One very regrettable observation must be made on this subject: in the country, as in the towns, craftsmanship is in decline. Techniques are becoming debased, traditions are gradually vanishing and the jewels still made by craftsmen in those centres which have preserved a certain activity, such as Tahala among the Ammeln, are very noticeably inferior in quality to the older pieces, even when the shape and decoration of these last are reproduced faithfully, which is not in fact always the case. Thus a folk tradition, which in the past was very rich and varied, is in decline. Ornaments produced towards the end of the last century still show it in its pure form.

The Berber woman in Plate 45 is dressed in a blue *izar*, which the Ammeln call *fidah*. The *fidah* is sometimes white, but it can also be — although this is much rarer — of black cotton edged with a coloured border.

The sandals, *idoukane*, are heavily embroidered.

(For details of the jewellery of the Anti-Atlas, see the appended pages of drawings).

When I went to Tiznit in the Chleuh country in 1936, it was a centre which had still retained something of its urban character.

CHLEUH DANCER FROM TIZNIT
PLATE 46

It is a stopping place on the way to the tribes of the western part of Morocco's deep south and is famous for its dancers, *chtahate*, and its singers, *chikhate*. These latter have a reputation for being pretty. They are above all extremely coquettish and, thanks to them, I was able to see assembled in one place the finest examples of the Berber jewellery of the Ida ou Semlal.

The local form of draped costume is the black *tamelhaft*, an overgarment drawn together at the waist by a simple brooch and pinned in front of the shoulders by means of enormous fibulae, *tizerzaï*, the biggest that I came across in Morocco, which stand out sumptuously against the black of the drapery. This example shows very clearly how much more important the decorative aspect of the jewel is than the functional. Size apart, the general pattern of this piece of jewellery is very similar to that of the *tizerzaï* of the valley of the Ammeln, but the two fibulae are so huge that the silver chain which normally links them cannot be used and is replaced by a little silk cord.

There are several different styles of headdress. These are always silver diadems, enriched with cloisonné enamels, enhanced with pendants and held in place by a system of little chains. The diadem worn by this *chtaha* is the *tassibba*, attached to a kerchief of gold silk brocade, *fechtoul*, which is held close to the head by a frontlet. Small chains support the large earrings with pendants, *ddouh*.

Among the numerous bracelets, the *nnbaïl* (sing.: *nnbala*), large flat rings with hinges, are bulky and always richly worked. Some of the ancient designs, which have now become very rare, are of an outrageous size, matching, both in scale and decoration, the huge anklets which used to be worn in the region and which have now been replaced with thin light bands of silver.

The *chtaha* shown here is wearing a thin white veil, *chane*, which is attached in a point to the head and floats gracefully as she dances.

In Tiznit, the *haïk* of the townswomen is not worn. It is replaced by a light blanket of white wool or cotton, the *amendil*, in which the women of Tiznit wrap the upper half of their bodies, draping it in an amusing way so that it comes to a point on the head, in a manner which reminds one very much of the *haïk* of Mogador. A small veil called *addal* is also worn. It is made of black or blue cotton and is decorated along the edges with brightly coloured embroidery, very like the *aferoual* of Tagmout.

At high altitudes in the Anti-Atlas, the mens' clothes are, during the cold weather, very similar to those of the Berbers of the Atlas. But the Chleuh, who live on the southern slopes of the mountain chain, have in part adopted the costume of the people of the far south and wear indigo blue clothes of Mauritanian influence. We will come back to these costumes again later.

One garment which is very typical of the folk culture of the Anti-Atlas, especially that of the Aït Ouaouzguit country, is the *akhnif* (pl.: *ikhnafen*) being worn by the shepherd in Plate 48. It is a black goat hair cloak, decorated with a broad reddish-orange half-moon, finely patterned. This magnificent piece of clothing is woven in a single piece and certain *ikhnafen* are real works of art. The orange coloured half-moon which decorates this cloak is explained in a number of ways. The most simple explanation would also seem to be the most logical: it is analogous to the well-known explanation of the patterns on carpets — it is said that the decoration represents a river flowing through a garden of flowers. From the hood, *aquelmoune*, hangs a large decorative tassel, *taouchkint*, and the *akhnif*, which has embroidery of the same colour on the breast, is edged with woollen fringes, *ichirabelaïn*. This cloak is worn by all the men, Muslims and Jews alike, and small-sized ones are made for the children. It is admired far beyond its place of origin. In the past, its use was more widespread than today and Charles de Foucauld noted in 1884 that it was «universally worn by the Glaoua, in the Dra, along the Souss basin and in the mountains of the Little Atlas.» It must be said that it is less frequently met with today. On the one hand there is an increasing tendency to abandon the manufacture of a garment the weaving of which requires a great deal of work. On the other, tourists like to bring back these magnificent objects as souvenirs and the Berbers, tempted by a quick profit, unfortunately do not hesitate to sell them.

Under the *akhnif*, can be seen the coarse woollen *haïk* of the mountain shepherd, who is also wearing slippers, *ijekjad*. These too are woven in a single piece, in the Ouaouzguit region on the appropriate small-sized looms. The local tradition of weaving, which in the recent past was extremely rich, appears in the characteristic geometric decoration, where repeated patterns of chevrons and lozenges make their appearance.

THE SAHARAN TRIBES
PRACTISING LONG-RANGE
NOMADISM

It was by setting out successively in various directions to the south of Goulimine and of the Bani mountains that I was able to find the Saharan nomads. They were members of the Aït Oussa, the Reguibat, the Ida ou Blel. They had all preserved their way of life in spite of the changes imposed by the passage of time. They are still passionately attached to their desolate country where their conditions of life are becoming increasingly difficult.

Of Berber origin, but completely Arabized at the time of the invasions of the Beni Hilal in the XIIIth and XIVth centuries, they speak a very pure and very classical variety of Arabic to the exclusion of any Berber dialect.

They live almost entirely on the produce of their camel herds, moving about in search of pasture between Mauritania and the plains of the Dra and between the Atlantic Ocean and the great sand dunes of the Algerian Sahara.

Until very recently, their poverty, their endurance, their love of adventure, made them real plunderers, true pirates of the desert. Formidable warriors, they were the masters of the western Sahara, forcing the commercial caravans to pay for the right of passage and pillaging whoever attempted to escape their control.

Those days are past. The justification for the camel caravans has dwindled away with the appearance of motor transport, and it is a long time since such piratical raids enabled them to supplement their normal means of subsistence.

Nevertheless, the traditions of long-range nomadism have survived in their love of wide-open spaces, coupled with their taste for life under the tent.

Here follow two typical examples of these nomads of the deep south: number 49 is a man of the Aït Moussa ou Ali, from the important Tekna group, which is half nomadic, half settled; number 50 is a long-range Saharan nomad of the Reguibat.

The Aït Moussa ou Ali, who form part of the great family of the Tekna, are to some extent settled. Many live in Goulimine, one of the «ports» on the northern shore of the Sahara where the camel caravans still flow in from Timbuktu and Mauritania, while others prepare to set out for the southern shore of the desert.

MAN OF THE AÏT MOUSSA OU ALI PLATE 49

The Tekna group is largely made up of Hilali Arabs, who have absorbed and assimilated some isolated pockets of Lemta Berbers.

While some of the Tekna are settled, or semi-nomadic, certain sub-groups, such as the Aït Moussa, live in tents, moving with their flocks over vast areas and owning big herds of camels. Their costume is very simple, very much like that of the Mauritanians with whom they are in contact. All wear the ample tunic called *qchaba* or *deréa*, like that being worn by the man of the Aït Moussa ou Ali in Plate 49.

It is made from a large piece of cotton cloth, measuring approximately 2.50 metres by 1.60 metres. An opening in the centre allows the passage of the head and it then hangs naturally down the length of the body, the two sides being simply knotted at the bottom or sewn upwards for a few centimetres. There is only one pattern for the *qchaba*, but it can be made from different materials and then takes the names of these: *bassaï* if it is of white cotton, *khount* if of ordinary blue cotton, *dimi* if of fine blue cotton, a luxury material woven in Mauritania; *bakha* if of linen cloth which, when richly embroidered in the manner of Sudanese clothing, is called *louakh*. Rich men wear several *qchacheb* one on top of the other. The sedentary peoples of the oases sometimes themselves adopt these garments and certain chiefs from the south of the Anti-Atlas wear blue embroidered *qchacheb* imported from Timbuktu. An *aselham* of white wool may complete the costume.

The headdress worn by the long-range nomads of the Sahara consists of a voluminous blue turban called *el haouli* or *aferoual*. All wear some amulet or other, *lahjeb*, about their necks and a small leather wallet, *kalb*; both objects are imported from Timbuktu, as is all the decorated leather work used in the region.

(See details of the *qchaba* in the appended pages of drawings.)

MAN OF THE REGUIBAT
PLATE 50

In the expanse of country occupied by the Tekna, one may come across settled peoples, semi-nomads and Saharan nomads. All wear the *qchaba*, but the way in which this piece of clothing is worn lends itself to numerous variations. It may be allowed to hang quite simply, as shown in Plate 49 or else it may be thrown back over the shoulders on either side.

For travelling, it is usual to wear it in the manner of the Reguibat of Plate 50. The true nomads of the Sahara draw it in at the waist with a belt, the drapery being held in place by means of two cords worn diagonally across the chest, from which are suspended the dagger, *koumiya*, and the satchel, *chqara*.

The bulky turban, *aferoual*, is made from a very long strip of blue *khent*. Each drapes it according to his personal taste, so as to create an individual style. It may also be thrown carelessly around the neck, leaving the abundant hair, which the Reguibat wear long and curled, free.

THE URBAN JEWS

I t would have been possible to show the Jewish costumes at the same time as those of the rural and urban peoples in the course of the various preceding chapters, for the Jewish population is completely integrated into Moroccan life in all its forms and in every area. However, the special features of this ethnic group have led me to deal with it separately.

When I arrived in Morocco in 1934, I had the good fortune to be able to observe, among the populations of the cities, the most beautiful and authentic traditional Jewish costumes before their use was abandoned, while in the oases of the south there still survived modes of dress straight out of the Bible.

My observations very naturally led me to take an interest in the origins and development of this ethnic group over the centuries, a history in which it either played a role or from which it suffered according to the region involved.

Before the beginning of the Christian era, the Tripolitanian Jews began to reach Barbary, but the great immigratory movement took place above all as a result of the exodus of the Jews from Palestine, which continued for centuries. This is described as the Judaeo-Berber period.

In the VIIth century, the arrival of the Arabs led to the Islamization of the Berber population, whereas the Jews refused to abjure their faith. It was not until the XIIIth century that they managed to have their religion recognized. Conditional on their paying a tax they were granted protected status, and they had to live in a district set aside for them — the *mellah* — generally built right next to the Sultan's palace, or that of the local authority.

After having shared with the Berbers the successive waves of the Arab invasion, they were to experience alternating periods of prosperity and repression in Muslim Morocco.

During periods of calm, this well accepted cohabitation even allowed certain Jews who exercised a high degree of influence with the Muslims to play a role in public affairs.

From the XVth century on, the Jewish population of Morocco received some new additions. The Jews of Andalusia were, like the Muslims, driven from Spain by the Christian reconquest. The *mellahs* of the north Moroccan towns increased considerably in size and the new wave of Jewish immigrants, spreading towards the interior of Morocco, came into contact with groups descended from Jews settled there since antiquity.

If I am here dwelling on the manner in which this peopling of the area took place, it is because it is illustrated in a very precise way by the clothes which I was able to see *in situ* and to record in my drawings at a moment in time when the way of life of these communities was evolving very rapidly and undergoing profound changes. The education given to the younger generations has made it possible for the more gifted to obtain first class jobs, not only in business, but also in the liberal professions.

It is easy to understand the inevitable effect of all this on the manner of dressing.

175

Thus I was able to observe, at one and the same time, old men wearing their long traditional gowns and living the life of their ancestors in the heart of the *mellah*, while the young people, living dynamic modern lives in the comfort of the new towns, were wearing the latest European fashions.

For greater clarity, I have chosen to divide the ten plates in this volume showing Jewish costume into two sections: five are devoted to urban dress, while the other five show the draped costumes still in use among the communities of the far south.

In Rabat, as elsewhere in the towns, traditional dress and European clothing coexist in the heart of the Jewish community. The women's clothing which I mainly encountered in the *mellah* consists of a sleeved bodice, *bata*, a long gathered skirt, often with flounces, *saya*, and a woollen shawl, *pagnouélo*.

The young girls usually wear ready-made dresses generally in bright colours.

For all of them, the headdress consists of a silk scarf, the same *sebniya roumiya* as that adopted today by all the urban Muslim women.

Tradition has been preserved in the ceremonial dress, *keswa el kbira*, worn by the bride and her relatives during the marriage rites. It is much the same in all the cities of Morocco. That of Rabat, worn by the Jewish woman in Plate 51, is the most splendid. It is a costume of an archaic cut which can be compared in many respects with certain European garments of the Middle Ages. It is entirely made of velvet, generally green or blue in the towns of the interior and garnet red in the cities of the coastal region and of the south.

The skirt, *zeltita* (that which wraps around), consisting of three broad panels, is a kind of wrap-around skirt crossing from left to right. It is decorated with numerous rows of gold braid. The bodice is very low cut with short sleeves, *rombaïz*, also lavishly decorated with braid, and fastens with little buttons of silver filigree down the plastron, which is made of the same velvet and covered with the kind of gold embroidery found on feast day sandals. Long wide muslin sleeves, *kmam tchmira*, are attached to the sleeves of the bodice. They are looped up behind and pinned on the shoulders and at the back. A big belt, *hzam*, made of thick gold brocade is folded in three and wrapped several times about the waist, being tied by means of the silk cordlets fastened to its ends.

As is the case in all traditional Jewish dress, special care is taken over the headdress and here it must be pointed out that an ancient Talmudic proscription forbade the Jewish women of the past from showing their hair after marriage. All brides were, therefore, compelled to hide their hair carefully under a headscarf, but certain exemptions, granted by some lenient rabbis, made it possible to remedy this absence of hair. These allowed the wearing of a wig, provided that it was not made from human hair. Thus there came into existence in the Jewish community, in Europe as in Africa, a very great variety of wigs in which the hair was replaced by an extraordinary range of substances: strips of cloth, woollen or silken thread, horse-hair or ostrich feathers.

Abandoned almost everywhere else today, the use of these wigs has been preserved in Morocco and one can see some curious examples in the *mellahs* of the oases of the south. The custom has almost entirely vanished in the towns, but a wig still forms part of the *keswa el kbira* — we see it here worn by the bride from Rabat. This is the *soualef*, two fringes of false hair made from threads of black silk, gathered into two plaits, *dlalat*, which hang down on either side of the face and in front of the shoulders.

The *soualef* is placed on top of the *fechtoul*, a long scarf of brocaded silk, which is tied tightly round the head, carefully hiding the hair. The *fechtoul* is caught in the belt and hangs down at the back as far as the heels. The fringes of the *soualef* are attached to a stiff band decorated with gold braid, which goes right round the head and is tied at the back by means of two cords. It in turn is covered by another *soualef* called the *soualef ez-zohar*, a sort of tiara which dips down slightly at the front and is covered with real pearls which serve as a background to arrangements of precious stones. The headdress is completed by a rich silken scarf with fringes, the ends of which hang down behind and which is tied in a point over the *soualef ez-zohar*. The sandals are the embroidered *chrabil* of the townswomen, called *rihiyat el kbar*.

The Jewish bride is always very heavily made up: her eyes darkened with *khol*, her cheeks red and her lips painted. She must wear an abundance of jewellery. The bride — like, for that matter, all the guests who surround her — is adorned with all the jewels she can lay her hands on, borrowed or rented if necessary.

Until recently, the custom of wearing this ancient form of dress for important ceremonies had been preserved. The father of the bride gave his daughter the *keswa el kbira* for her marriage and she would continue to wear it throughout her life for important festivities: marriages, circumcisions, etc. The *soualef ez-zohar* did not form part of this costume. A very valuable ornament, it was owned by only a few rich families in Rabat who, however, would lend it very willingly to new brides within the *mellah*. Today, the tradition is rapidly being lost and women wear this ancient costume for the major festivals only in the old conservative families. They then most commonly wear their grandmother's costumes.

(For the various pieces which make up the *keswa el kbira*, see the appended pages of drawings.)

The formal dress worn in the past in all the cities of Morocco, has, as we have said, very few variants. It is, however, to be observed that the bride of Fez in Plate 52 shows a decided difference in the cut of her *rombaïz*, which is widely open at the front.

JEWISH BRIDE OF FEZ
PLATE 52

The muslin sleeves are much shorter than those of Rabat and are worn folded back above the elbow and pinned to the inner side of the short sleeves of the bodice. Finally, the decoration of braid and lace is, on the whole, much more discreet, especially as regards the «wrap-around skirt». As they all do, however, this has a stylized hand, *khamsa*, embroidered on the side, to preserve the bride from the evil eye. The costumes from Tétouan are richest in braids and embroideries.

The headdress is less splendid at Fez than at Rabat: no elaborate tiaras, just a mounting called *sfifa* to which is attached long false hair of silk, which is divided into two broad bands that fall at the back onto the shoulders. A folded silk handkerchief, *khtib*, closely follows the shape of the *sfifa* and is tied at the back.

The face of the Jewish bride from Fez, like her Arab counterpart, is decorated with little red and white dots.

In Plate 52, the shape of the *rombaïz* indicates that it is akin to the *keswa el kbira* worn by the Jewish women of Oran and Algiers, who also belong to the groups of Jews driven out of Spain. And everywhere Spanish names appear for the various pieces of clothing (*pounta* and *peto* for the front of the bodice or plastron, *geraldeta*, *zeltita* for the skirt).

It is also interesting to note that in the past the Jewish women veiled themselves just like their Muslim counterparts. «Married women never go out unless wrapped up in their *haïk*», noted Dr Lemprière during his journey in 1791. Indeed, Jewish women continued to hide their faces in their great shawls, *pagnouelo*, long after that.

The festival costume of this Jewish woman of Tiznit, a large straggling village in the south of the Chleuh country, shows some of the traditional character of the *keswa el kbira* of the towns of the north. It is very interesting to note that thanks

JEWISH WOMAN OF TIZNIT
PLATE 53

177

to the survival of this very characteristic piece of clothing, one can reconstitute the immigration route taken by the Andalusian Jews entering Morocco from the XVth century on.

Naturally the first *mellahs* to welcome the newcomers were those of the cities in the north of the country: Tangiers, Tétouan, then Rabat, Meknes, Fez.

The great wave of immigrants next reached Marrakesh, where I was still able to find a large number of *keswa el kbira*, just as I did on the coast down which the immigration descended by way of Mogador and Safi as far as Tiznit. There, inevitably, the southward movement came to a halt and, instead, turned eastwards, penetrating the heart of the Anti-Atlas, where indeed the same Andalusian-style costumes are found in the major *mellahs*, such as those of Talaïnt, Ifrane and Tahala.

These are not exact copies of the *keswa el kbira*. The bodice and front are the same — the same cut, the same abundance of gold braid. It is known as *qaftane*. The skirt, on the other hand, is the same shape as the *saya*, cut from a rich silk or velvet, embellished by a flounce. It is here too called *zeltita*.

Thus, it is possible to see in a tangible form the exact point where the immigrants from Spain, who are often called *forasteros*, and the Jews of ancient Hebrew stock met. The women of this latter group, as we will see further on, always wear cotton materials, which they drape in exactly the same way as the indigenous populations among whom they live.

The Jewish woman of Tiznit in Plate 53 is dressed in a costume which clearly illustrates its close relationship with the *keswa el kbira*.

Something which is most particular to this region is the very pretty hairstyle. It consists of a wig, a splendid piece of local craftsmanship, called the *tijajin d'mahdouh* — a wig intended as always to hide the hair of a married woman.

This headdress, which completely covers the head, is made of silver threads interwoven with hair from the tails of cows. The cloth thus produced is some 12 to 15 centimetres in width and from it escape the hairs, parted into two locks which overlap slightly onto the upper part of the forehead. The most beautiful are decorated with five transversal straps of silver and cloisonné enamel.

Over the wig, which is held in place by means of cords at the back, is pinned a scarf of red silk brocaded in gold, the *fechtoul*, which is allowed to float freely behind. The overall effect is charming and recalls the grace of the hennin worn in medieval Europe. The Jewish woman does not remove her *mahdouh* while going about her daily chores. Similarly, she wears at all times the greater part of her jewellery and in particular the very ancient and heavy *tanbalt*, here seen in profile. At the great festivals, the women almost collapse under the weight of their ornaments. Let us also remember that here we are very close to the cradle of the jeweller's craft, both Jewish and Berber, to the Ida ou Semlal of the Chleuh.

This festival costume is worn in all the *mellahs* of the Anti-Atlas. Beyond this point, further to the south, I only came across Jewish women draped in white cotton, exactly like the local Berber draperies.

JEWISH TOWN-DWELLER
PLATE 54

Plate 54 shows a Jewish town-dweller. It is the dress of a well-to-do man and, in this particular case, of a rabbi. This costume for indoor wear does not vary from one town to another.

After the Islamization of Morocco, Jewish men came to wear the same out-door dress as the Muslims — the *jellaba*. This has become so much the rule that it is worn everywhere but, up until very recently, the Jews were obliged by law to dress entirely in black.

During a journey in 1859, the Abbé Godard observed «the colour green is the prerogative of the *chérifs* and bright colours are forbidden to the Jews. Their headdress is a black cap held on by a kerchief: it was at Morocco (i.e. Marrakesh) and at Méquinez that they first won the right to wear this kerchief in order to protect their ears. In actual fact, they wanted to spare themselves the insults of the Moorish children, who would amuse themselves by pulling off their caps. They do not have the right to tie this kerchief under the chin with a double knot; the knot must be single and the kerchief removed in the presence of the Muslim authorities. They are always obliged to wear a black cloak. Furthermore, this cloak must be worn with the opening slightly to the right and the hood falling on the left shoulder, so as to impede movement, another mark of servitude. »

The «cloak» mentioned by the Abbé Godard is the *jellaba*. The traditional Jew wears under this garment the indoor clothes shown in Plate 54, while the others have adopted European dress. Over the shirt, the trousers, *seroual*, are worn, a waist-coat decorated with braid, *bedaiya*, and a sort of tunic in woollen cloth, *joukha*, held in at the waist by means of a silk sash, *kerziya*.

For special occasions, he wears a second waistcoat, not buttoned, and another tunic which takes the place of an overgarment and does not close. This costume, when it is not black, is always dark. Only the silk *kerziya* is of a bright colour.

The headdress is the classic black *chachiya* set quaintly on the back of the head. I was still able to see a few old men who covered it with a handkerchief, generally blue or black with white spots. The sandals, which in the past were always black, are today frequently replaced by the yellow *blari* used by the Muslims.

(For details of the *joukha*, see the appended pages of drawings.)

THE JEWISH COMMUNITIES OF SOUTHERN MOROCCO

Small, very ancient Jewish communities exist in most of the oases of southern Morocco, from the Tafilelt to the Atlantic. It is difficult to be precise about their origins. One can only posit that they are what remains of the Jewish population from Palestine which emigrated to Morocco during the first centuries of the Christian era. It is impossible not to be astonished that these tiny communities should have been able to survive, perpetuating their religion in its most archaic form, and avoiding extermination by those who appeared to wish to destroy everything that resisted Islam, when their small numbers seemed to make it inevitable that they should disappear.

If in the past, the Jews of these small communities were secretly under the protection of the tribes among whom they lived, compelled to pay them an annual tribute, it was nevertheless not unusual for a rich Jewish notable to play a certain political role in the community in which he lived, thanks to his fortune and his intelligence. This was so, for example, in the case of Mouchi n'Aït Mijo, the *cheikh* of the Jews of Beni Sbih, who wielded considerable influence in the Ktaoua — in the Dra valley — at the beginning of the century.

Moreover, according to traditions piously preserved in the *mellahs*, the Jewish inhabitants of the south are said to have played an important political role in the past.

Certain writers add support to these hypotheses; but what is more certain, coming closer to our own times, is that the Tafilelt and the Dra were important centres of Jewish culture. From the end of the IXth century, their *mellahs*, proud of their doctors and their scholars, joined with that of Fez in disputing the intellectual supremacy of the Jews of Kairouan. In the XIIth century, under the Almohad dynasty, the Jews of the Dra and of the Tafilelt were victims of a first persecution, which put an end to their intellectual and religious movement. Moïse Abraham Halevy the Draouï, a talented writer, a well-known scholar and a doctor by profession, was obliged to leave his country and take refuge in the East.

When, in 1935-36, I had the great good fortune to encounter a number of these communities, they were for the most part engaged in such crafts, often poorly remunerated but useful to the whole local population, as blacksmiths, packsaddle-makers, cobblers, grocers and jewellers.

These very small Jewish communities live in a *mellah* inside the *ksar* inhabited by the sedentary Quebala. Over the centuries they have preserved their autonomy and their own special codes of behaviour: they have a village council presided over by a *cheikh*, a school where all the male children learn to read and write in accordance with Talmudic tradition. The scrupulous observation of their customs and their religious formalism makes these rural Jews the closest to the Hebrews of ancient times.

A study of the clothing leads one to think that these residual communities are still as they were before the Islamization of the country, when they and the indigenous Berbers formed an association of groups collectively described as «Judaeo-Berber».

In all these communities, the Jewish women are faithful to the ancestral custom of wearing draped costume, and faithful even to the local variations in this, which changes according to the Berber tribes among which they live. This faithfulness, thus perceptible in tangible form, is a reflection of their attachment to the past in all its aspects.

This is why Plates 55 to 60 constitute precious documents concerning these small social groups, witnesses to an extremely remote past, which are now abruptly confronted by external forces which will hasten their disappearance.

In 1935, I was one of the first Frenchmen to enter the Tafilelt region and I was able to go down the valley of the Ziz, as far as Erfoud and Rissani, the southern-most points of the pre-Saharan palm groves.

I came from Ksar es Souk, where I had been able to draw a man of the Aït Khalifa. There, in the heart of the Tafilelt, I was privileged to find a people who had been preserved from outside influences.

Erfoud was founded on the very site of the ancient Sijilmassa, the starting point of the caravans which linked central Africa to the towns of northern Morocco. It was an important commercial crossroads where Jewish merchants played a very active role. At the moment when I arrived there the *mellah* was still very much alive. It was truly enchanting to see the Jewish women dressed in their traditional costumes, going about their affairs against an almost Biblical background.

I have chosen the woman of Erfoud, Plate 55, as a characteristic example of the Jewish women of the Tafilelt. She is descended from the group of Jews who were the very first to immigrate. She wears the same draped costume as her most remote ancestors. She often wears red, a colour frequently adopted in the *mellahs* of the south-east along the fringes of the Sahara. The length of cloth is used in the same way as the Berber *izar* and is called *khelali*. It is fastened in front of the shoulders by two fibulae, generally small in size. For work, they are replaced by a system of tying: the two thicknesses of cloth to be joined are placed together over a small pebble and around this a cord is tied, enclosing it in a little bag as used for herbs in cooking.

The *khelali* is draped over a shirt of a special cut called *déréa*. This is also made of red cotton and its long sleeves are bell-shaped and very wide. They are turned back and pinned on the shoulders so that they do not reach down below the elbows. The front of the *déréa* and the insides of the sleeves, which is the visible part, are decorated with green and yellow embroidery, worked according to a pattern with geometric designs which have not changed since time immemorial.

The hairstyle is very original and is composed of *groune* (horns). It is a hairstyle also found in the *mellahs* of Bou Denib and Colomb-Béchar. It is formed of two hanks of thick wool arranged one on either side of the head, tightly bound round and held in a horizontal position by means of a system of small plaits which enlace them. The horns thus formed are finally secured by several bands of cloth and are covered by a cap, *bniqa*, of embroidered cotton, or, on great occasions, brocade. The point of the *bniqa* is folded backwards. A silk frontlet, *mehammel*, covers the forehead. A fringed silk kerchief, *sebniya del réta*, is pinned on top of everything, with the ends falling behind. When she goes out, as this plate shows, the Jewish woman of Erfoud places, over her headdress, a great veil of white muslin, the centre of which is decorated with a scattering of small woven flowers. She can, if she so wishes, wrap herself in this light veil, or let it float free. The origin of the *groune* added to the wig is certainly very ancient; it is said that it is linked to the superstition of the horn, a talisman against the evil eye, which is also found in the headdress of some Jewish women in Tunisia and the Balkans. One might also wonder whether it doesn't represent a survival from the far-off cult of Isis, whose horns were the symbol of fertility, for it is a fact that the *groune* are always added to Jewish women's headdresses on the day of their marriage, the day from which, like their urban counterparts, they must hide their hair from view. We are quite definitely dealing here with a wig, an object which has been the pretext in the *mellahs* of the far south of Morocco for some rather extraordinary combinations, as we shall see in the case of the Jewish women of Goulmima and Tinehrir.

In the Tafilelt it is traditional for children who have barely reached puberty to marry and hence the bridegroom is sometimes very young, like the one we have shown in Plate 56.

JEWISH BRIDEGROOM OF THE TAFILELT
PLATE 56

The costume is very uniform in style and its various components are decorated with matching embroideries. They are worked in red and black, in chain stitch and in feather stitch, and bear a rather strange resemblance to the folk embroidery of central Europe. Over the long-legged *seroual* is worn the *déréa*, a shirt with wide sleeves, very heavily worked. An embroidered cap, *tarbouch*, completes the outfit. The belt, *hezam nemri*, is made of thick brocade, urban in origin, from the workshops of Fez.

The extraordinary resemblance between the motifs embroidered on this garment and the analogous decorations on shirts and blouses from the Balkans is to be found in other *mellahs* in the south of Algeria and Tunisia. This is clear proof of a diaspora which scattered its colonies far and wide, carrying with it the same decorative motifs stamped with the evidence of Byzantine influence.

Between the Tafilelt, where the Wadi Ziz flowing down from the peaks of the Atlas ends at Erfoud, and Ouarzazate, where one meets up with the road which leads across the Atlas from south to north to reach Marrakesh, there are numerous oases inhabited by sedentary Quebala, whose costumes are represented in Plates 32 to 34.

JEWISH WOMAN OF GOULMIMA
PLATE 57

Towns or villages have grown up wherever the watercourses, coming down from the mountain range, have made it possible to tend palm groves and agricultural land. To each of the oases of any importance, a *mellah* has been attached, inhabited, as in the Tafilelt, by Jews who have been there since the remotest times.

The oasis of Goulmima is located at the entry of the Wadi Rheris, a watercourse parallel to the valley of the Ziz. Here, we again find the draped *khelali*, usually red as in the Tafilelt. The garment is the same, but the hairstyle, often of a very strange shape, completely changes the overall appearance. When I arrived in this part of the deep south of Morocco in 1935, I was able to observe the details of the various headdresses, which appeared to me to be vestiges of traditions which were very unusual and very ancient, but on the verge of disappearing.

In Goulmima, the headdress again has as its basis the wig, which must hide the hair. Here, as at Erfoud, it is an enormous edifice, on top of which is placed the *soualef*. Amply wound about with turban-like wrappings, it includes a principal headband to which hair made from black wool is attached, which falls in two plaits on either side.

Two horns, the *groune*, also form part of the composition of this headdress, consisting of two long thick rolls of heavy wool, falling towards the rear on either side above the shoulders.

Here again, the big white shawl is placed over the headdress. It is of light muslin,

183

often striped with bands of silk, and serves as a kind of demi-*haïk* in which a woman can wrap herself more or less completely.

I never saw the Jewish women of Goulmima wearing any of the golden jewels which I had observed at Erfoud. The silver fibulae are the same as those worn by the women of the Quebala. To the right hand one is pinned a thick cloth used when transporting water. It is folded up on top of the shoulder before setting the jar there.

Like all the women of the fringe Saharan peoples, the Jewish women of the oases of the south have a predilection for large amber necklaces. The one to be seen in this plate, the *mezroua*, is embellished with inverted silver crosses, *tiour*, reminiscent of Tuareg jewellery, placed between the spherical amber beads.

Two curled side pieces, composed of solid silver and very heavy, hang in front of the ears, simply suspended from the headband by a cord.

(For details of the Jewish wig of Goulmima, see the appended pages of drawings.)

Between Goulmima and the valley of the Dadès, lies the Todrha region, whose centre is the oasis of Tinehrir. The Jewish women there have adopted the draped dress as it is worn by the women of the Ahel Todrha.

We have described the details of this method of draping in Plate 32. Here it is shown covering each shoulder in turn to produce a crossed over effect at the back as well as in front. But more usually, the Jewish women, instead of letting the drapery float free, catch it in at the waist with a handkerchief which takes the place of a belt, as in Plate 58.

The traditional headdress of the Jewish women of Tinehrir is the most astonishing wig to be found in all the *mellahs* of Morocco. It is made of a large number of cows' tails arranged side-by-side so as to form two enormous swathes which give the surprising appearance of a very high cap.

This heavy wig is embellished along its central parting with a line of small ornaments.

In the valley of the Dadès, very different tribes live side-by-side and among them certain sub-groups of the Aït Atta play an important role. The Quebala look after the oases, and to them have been attached a whole chain of highland *mellahs*, among them those of Kelaa of the Mgouna and of Tiilit, whose costume is shown in Plate 59.

The method of draping is identical to that of the Aït Atta, but only white cotton is used; Jewish women do not wear blue *khent*. The wig is reduced to a very small size; it is covered by a diadem, *tasfift*, a high quality piece of jewellery made by craftsmen. It is a crown of considerable size, composed of little silver plates decorated with repoussé work and engraving, which overlap and are sewn on to a piece of leather or thick material. The *tasfift* is set on top of a long scarf of burgundy red silk striped with brilliant colours, which is none other than the *toukaït* worn also by the Berber women on the southern slopes of the Atlas.

Among the numerous necklaces made with large spherical amber beads which are worn in the valley, one sometimes sees distinctive ancient examples such as the one worn by this Jewish woman of Tiilit, in which amber beads alternate with plaques of worked silver.

The other jewels, fibulae, bracelets and rings, are the same as those worn by the Ahel Dadès.

The Jewish women share the same customs as the Berber women of the valley as regards facial decoration. Here, it is not a question of tattoos, but of patterns painted in black, using *harquous*, and in red, using *aker*.

184

The Dra valley, which is the most important valley of southern Morocco, is rendered fertile by water coming down from the High Atlas. In former times, as the Wadi Dra passed in front of the desert plains of the Hammada it made a large bend before heading for the Atlantic. Today, the valley is only fertile as far as Tagounit; Mhamid marks the edge of the area which has become desert.

In Plates 35, 36 and 37 we saw the Berber and *harratine* inhabitants of the central part of this valley. It was beyond Zagora, in the Ktaoua, that I came across the most typical Jewish dress, particularly in the *mellahs* of Tamgrout and Beni-Sbih. This woman of the Beni-Sbih was the wife of a very rich man of the region. Her dress shows, in its irreproachable authenticity, the appearance of the most ancient costumes.

Here, the set of jewels is complete. The fibulae called *khelalat*, as in the north, are skilfully engraved and embellished with silver plaques, *mraïat* (mirrors). The earrings are immense and actually transfix the main body of the ear. Each is adorned with three great rings made of real pearls, precious stones and tiny gold beads, *saaïr*.

No wig is worn in the Dra valley. The hair is covered by a silk scarf held in place by a system of little chains, the *talgamout* with its innumerable pendants, which we have already seen in the Chleuh country. The temples are hidden by large curls made of ostrich feathers.

The necklaces are not made exclusively of special amber beads. They are made of a variety of stones in pretty colours. Some are real collectors' pieces.

The large bracelets are called *mesmout*; the small ones, of Sudanese inspiration, are called *mefokh*.

Here again, it is to be noted that the draped costumes worn by the Jewish women of the extreme south of Morocco are identical to those worn by the Berber women. Not the slightest trace of Spanish influence can be found in the clothes of this region. The great veil of cotton and wool, or cotton and silk, is woven locally.

The costume worn by the Jewish men in the *mellahs* of the Atlas and of the south does not merit any special mention. Their clothes are, generally speaking, very similar to those of the Berbers among whom they live. They are, however, very easily recognized by their little black *chachiya* and also by their *nouader*, long sidelocks which they allow to hang down in front of their ears.

When travelling, some wear the black *jellaba*, like the urban members of their faith.

EXPLANATION OF THE PRINCIPAL WAYS OF DRAPING THE HAÏK AMONG ARAB TOWNSWOMEN
PLATE A

N.B. — The dimensions of the *haïk* are not fixed. They can vary slightly, depending on the taste and stature of the wearer. The measurements given here, merely for guidance, apply to persons of normal body size.

1 to 5. — Method of draping the *haïk* at Rabat and Salé (see Plate 6).

1 — The *haïk* is folded back upon itself by about 40 centimetres along its length: in this way its height can be regulated, since it should reach down to the feet. One end is brought forward over the left shoulder and tied at the side in front to a big solidly knotted pleat called *mechmoum* (the bunch of flowers) which takes up about 1 metre of cloth.

2. — The rest of the material is passed round to the back, and above the head.

3. — The end which is hanging down on the right side, again folded over upon itself so as to adjust the height, is gathered up into a big fold, mirroring the *mechmoum* on the left, and is held under the right arm. There should be the same fullness on either side.

4. — The two sides of the *haïk* are brought forwards with the hands so as to cover the face, allowing the use of only one eye. Prior to this the face has been covered by means of the *litham* or *ngab*, a scarf one end of which binds the forehead, while the other envelops the lower part of the face, leaving only the eyes visible.

5. — The appearance of the draping from the side.

6 to 8. — Method of draping the *haïk* at Fez.

6. — With her *haïk*, folded over on itself as before so as to adjust the height, the woman wraps herself in a loop of about 2.50 metres. The two «bunches of flowers» are made and tied one on each side to keep the *haïk* up round the waist. These two «bunches of flowers» are held by a long band of cloth, *tekka*, which passes round behind the nape of the neck and hangs down sufficiently low on either side to be visible once the draping is complete.

7. — The rest of the cloth is taken backwards over the head.

8. — The hands roll the two sides of the *haïk* and adjust it at the temples; it is then held in place by the left hand alone. Both eyes and part of the *ngab* remain visible. The right hand remains free.

9 to 10. — Method of draping the *haïk* at Marrakesh.

9. — In Marrakesh, the *haïk* is most commonly adjusted and held in place at the waist simply by means of a belt *mdomma*. Extra fullness is provided by a pleat at the waist on the left side only. The *haïk* then passes, in the usual way, backwards over

the head, but the end, which is longer than in the other towns, is brought back again (with the material still folded over on itself) from right to left, thus doubling the amount of material over the head.

10. — The right side is brought across on top of the left one and both are held in place by means of the left hand, while the right hand is used to maintain a triangular opening.

11 to 15. — Draping the *battaniyya* (the form of drapery known as *chedda wé radda*). The *battaniyya* is a large woollen blanket, roughly 1.80 metres by 5.50 metres. It can be draped like any urban *haïk*, but is often worn by women little concerned with local tradition, or by village women who have come to town, in the following manner:

11. — The *battaniyya* is folded over on itself lengthwise and thrown over the head and arms.

12. — The two ends are thrown back with a rapid movement of the forearms.

13. — The right end is folded over onto the head.

14. — The left end is in its turn thrown onto the head, on top of the right end.

15. — The volume of material on top of the head is considerable. This is the appearance produced by this method of draping as seen from a three-quarter rear view. This technique makes it possible for the women to drape themselves very quickly.

16 to 18. — Method of draping the *haïk* at Mogador

16. — The *haïk* worn in Mogador is generally a long woollen blanket similar to the *battaniyya*, with transversal blue stripes at the end. It is first attached under the arms and the rest of the material goes twice round the head.

17. — The striped end hangs down in front. The drapery over the head takes on a pointed appearance.

18. — Properly draped, there should be three large folds at the back.

19 to 20. — Method of draping the *tamelhaft* at Taroudant.

The draped costume of Taroudant, known as *tamelhaft*, takes the place both of the Berber *izar* (see the plate showing the Berber draped costumes) and of the urban *haïk*.

19. — Fastened in front of the shoulders, by two fibulae called *khellalat*, it is then taken straight back over the head, without being held by a belt.

20. — The free end, folded back on itself widthwise, is still ample enough for the woman to be able to veil herself completely in the usual manner of the *haïk*, as can be seen in Plate 7.

EXPLANATION OF THE PRINCIPAL FORMS OF BERBER DRAPERY — PLATE B

1 to 5. — Method of draping the *izar* in the Middle Atlas.

The Berber draped costume, generally called *izar*, may be of either cotton or wool and in principle is worn directly over the naked body. It can also be draped over the *toubit*, a kind of long chemise which buttons down the front, and even occasionally over the *qaftane*, in those places where some Berber women have adopted this urban piece of clothing. In this last case, the material used is generally a light imported cloth, often a transparent silk-type stuff with a brocaded decoration.

1. — The *izar* is folded over on itself lengthwise, to a varying extent, depending on the height to be given to the draped dress. One end is brought forwards over the left shoulder; a large loop is formed with the material on the right side.

2. — Two silver fibulae, which have different names in the different dialects, are used to pin the back part of the cloth to the front, a wide opening being left for the right arm.

3. — The rest of the *izar* is brought round behind over the head. The woman then catches the *izar* at the waist with a belt, which goes under the overhanging fold. The draped costume is thus adjusted and fixed in position.

4. — The appearance of the *izar* when finally adjusted. The dotted line shows where the belt is. Depending on the region, the *izar* may come down to the feet, or only to mid-calf. (see Plates 20, 21, 22, etc.)

5. — The woman may bring the fold which hangs down over her belt at the back forwards over her head. She may also use this fold to carry her child or any other kind of load.

6. — Method of draping of a Chaouïa woman

As in sketch n° 5, this woman has brought the back panel of her draperies forwards over her head. Here the material used is a thick woollen blanket, but the technique is the same.

7 to 9. — Method of draping the *izar* in the Todrha (see Plate 32).

This technique of draping is peculiar to the women of the Ahel Todrha. The *izar*, which measures roughly 5 metres by 1.30 metres, is attached on top of the shoulders not with fibulae, but by knots; a little pebble or fruit stone is enclosed within the two layers of cloth to be joined and tied round with a string. A large loop of about 1.60 metres is left on the right side.

8. — The rest of the *izar* is brought round behind to form another loop, also of about 1.60 metres on the left side.

9. — From the two knots on the shoulders hangs a fold of about 0.40 to 0.50 metres. The draped costume thus obtained crosses over in front and at the back and hangs free, without being held in at the waist by a belt. It is always white and is worn over a black *toubit*.

10 to 11. — Method of draping the *izar* among the Glaoua.

10. — In a part of the Atlas and the Anti-Atlas (among the Glaoua and as far as Siroua), the *izar* is draped by bringing the two sides of the upper part together in the middle of the chest, where they are pinned together to form a sort of little cape.

11. — This draped costume is thus crossed at the back. The *izar* worn in this manner is usually made of *khent*, an indigo blue cotton cloth.

12 to 15. — Method of draping found in the western Atlas and in the Dra valley.

This is a reduplicate draped costume, of which there are many different varieties in the south. It is worn on top of another *izar* which may be equally well white or blue.

12. — This draped costume consists of a length of white woollen cloth measuring roughly 1.30 metres by 4.50 metres, in which the woman wraps herself up completely.

13. — The back section of material is brought over the head and the front part is held between the teeth, then the whole is held in position at the waist by a belt.

14. — Once the draperies have been put in position, here is the effect obtained by bringing the upper part onto the shoulders.

15. — By letting the upper part drop, the woman can show off her first *izar*; the second then looks rather like several very bulky skirts on top of each other. (This last sketch is of a woman of the Mesguita in the Dra, where the first *izar* is always of indigo cotton.)

16. — *Tashdat*, the reduplicate draped costume of the Aït Atta.

This shows how the two breadths of cloth, one white and one blue which go to form the double *izar* described in the commentary to Plate 30 cross over. Each panel measures 2.75 metres by 1.30 metres.

This method of draping is found both in the Dadès and in the Dra valley, wherever sub-divisions of the Aït Atta are living. It is worn with the veil seen on the woman in Plate 33.

17. — Reduplicate draped costume of the *hartaniate* of the Dra.

This is another form of double draped costume. Here both widths of cloth are of the full size (approx. 5 metres by 1.40 metres). They are superimposed in such way that the white of the underneath one appears wherever a section is folded over.

18. — *Izar* of the Aït Morrhad

Made of *khent*, or sometimes of white cotton for feast days, the *izar* of the Aït Morrhad is one of the most classic draped costumes of Morocco. The width of the material is sufficient for the draped dress to reach the feet even when the upper folds also fall quite low (see Plate 28).

19. — *Tamizart* of the Zemmour, also called *tahandirt*.

The woman in Plate 21 is wearing the *izar* on its own. Here is how the women of the Zemmour wear their *tamizart*, which is larger than those of the neighbouring tribes.

20. — *Tizakouine* of the Issafène.

This is how the *tizakouine*, already shown in Plate 43, may be worn so as to completely cover the head. Like their Aït Abd Allah neighbours (see Plate 42), the women sometimes use the tassels to create an original headdress.

21. — *Taberdouat* of the Aït Bahr.

This woman of the Aït Bahr, a sub-division of the Aït Jellidasen (see Plate 23) is wearing the *taberdouat* under her arms, held up by means of two cords which serve as shoulder straps. This is the custom in the Aït Ouarrain group.

22. — *Khenita* of the Aït Atta of the Reteb.

This is how the extremely prudish women of the Aït Atta of the Reteb wear the veil called *khenita*, described in the commentary to Plate 29.

23. — Small Berber veil of cotton called *achdat* (in the Atlas) or *takhardit* (in the Dra valley).

In summer, the Berber women frequently leave off their woollen cloaks, replacing them with this rectangle of cotton material of variable dimensions, with which they cover their heads.

DETAILS OF MALE URBAN DRESS — PLATE C

N.B. — No detailed sketch has been given of the *qaftane*, since the cut is the same for men and for women (see the plates of details of female urban dress).

1. — *Tchamir* (see the commentary to Plate 1). All garments with sleeves, whatever they may be and whether for men or for women, show a gradual evolution in shape (fullness and cut of the sleeves). The changes taking place in all these garments are analogous to those affecting the *qaftane*.

2. — *Farajiya* (see the commentary to Plate 1).

3. — *Foqiya* (see the commentary to Plate 1). Made of a very light material, the *foqiya* is mainly worn instead of the *jellaba*. It is part of everyday wear for nicely dressed little boys.

4 to 6. — *Keswa del mahsour* (see Plate 3 and commentary).

4. — *Mental*, also called *kebbout*.

5. — *Bdaiyat*. This waistcoat has a little pocket at the side for the watch.

6. — *Seroual*. The cut of the *seroual* shown here is that of the modern *keswa del mahsour*, which is of Algerian origin. The old-fashioned cut was different: the trousers had the form of a long rectangle with a band of material, *tekka*, serving as a draw-string at the waist (the woman's *seroual* is made in this way).

7. — *Seroual* being worn, seen from behind. One can see the sort of pouch which is formed at the back between the legs, due to the generous amount of cloth in the centre of this type of trousers.

8. — *Jellaba* (See plate 1 and commentary). This shows the classic cut. The modern *jellaba* is narrower and has sleeves which are also narrower as well as being longer. The old fashioned style of *jellaba*, which had wide sleeves, had two openings at the level of the arms so that the forearms could be disengaged for performing the ablutions without removing the garment. A slit at the front of the chest brought the number of openings in this garment to seven, thus giving rise to a joke in which it is compared to hell («hell with its seven gates»).

It is interesting to note that the ample cut of Arab clothing is not, in the opinion of the learned, a practical matter (for example so that they should be airy and thus protect against the heat), but one of religion: the good Muslim should be ready at any moment for prayer, which is carried out so often during the course of the day, and hence wears clothes which modestly hide the form of the body while at the same time possessing the fullness required by the prostrate positions adopted.

9. — The *selham* seen from the side.

10 to 14. — Various examples of urban male headgear.

10. — *Tarbouch tassa* (literally *tarbouch* in the shape of a bowl). This *tarbouch* of red wool is the most common headwear.

11. — *Rezza del qaleb* (literally *rezza* made on a mould). This *rezza* is in fact rolled around the *tarbouch* which has first been placed on a wooden mould. It is a delicate operation left to hairdressers who, in accordance with strictly observed custom (*caïda*), roll a long piece of light muslin, dampened with water so that it lends itself better to the process, around the *tarbouch*. The *rezza del qaleb* obtained in this way is the headwear of the well-to-do middle class and of men-of-letters.

12. — The headdress of the chief of the *moghazni* in the Sultan's palace. It is the classic *chachiya* of the *Maghzen* (see Plate 4), covered with a very large *rezza del qaleb*. In the Sultan's palace, all the officials from the humblest to the most important wear the *chechiya*. The *moghazni* wear it on its own. The chief officials wear it surrounded by a turban, the size of which increases according to the importance of their rank. In the past, the viziers and high officials wore enormous turbans, covered by a scarf, *amama*. Today, they simply wear whatever *rezza del qaleb* suits their taste, leaving the very noticeable prerogative of bulky turbans to the chiefs of the *moghazni*. The headdress shown in sketch 12 requires two 40 yard lengths of fine muslin (the material is imported from England). The tassel of blue silk, *choucha*, is held down by the layers of muslin. It is worn with this on the right.

13. — *Tarbouch misri*. This *tarbouch* is of Egyptian origin and is worn principally by elegant young men.

14. — *Taguiya*, a knitted woollen cap. Of Berber origin, it has lately reached the town. Well-to-do men are happy to wear it indoors, whereas working men use it as their everyday headgear. It is also often worn by little boys.

15 to 17. — Three classic types of Moroccan dagger. The dagger is worn less and less in town and the craftsmen now make only indifferent copies of the ancient models, the principal types of which are shown here.

15. — *Sboula*, a dagger with a straight blade, the engraved silver sheath of which has at its centre a sleeve of velvet embroidered in gold or silver thread. The Moroccan dagger is worn slung diagonally across the body on a silken cord, *mejdoul*, attached to its rings.

16. — *Koummiya*, the most ancient type, widespread in the south and especially in the Anti-Atlas. It is very clearly reminiscent of the ancient Persian dagger. The outer face is richly decorated in relief, while the inner face is of copper with some rudimentary engraving.

17. — *Khanjer*. Of finely engraved silver, sometimes embellished with enamels, this is the most massive of the daggers. It is the preferred weapon of the great chiefs of the North Atlas.

18. — *Chkara*, leather satchel slung from the shoulder diagonally across the body on a cord. There are numerous models in varying degrees of luxury. It is an indispensable accessory to Moroccan traditional dress, since only the *seroual* has pockets.

19 to 24. — Method of draping the *ksa* (see Plate 2 and commentary).

19. — One end is attached to the belt, then the *ksa* is passed backwards over the left shoulder, brought round to the front, then over the head, forming a large loop.

20. — The upper part of the material making this loop is folded forwards over the left shoulder.

21 and 22. — What remains of the material is taken up and again brought forwards over the left shoulder in the same movement as before (when the *ksa* is less long, only one of these two movements is carried out, but the thickness of the cloth gathered on the shoulder gives fullness and contributes to the noble appearance of the draping).

23. — The front part has now been carefully rolled at the level of the waist. The end which was hanging down to the right, held in position under the chin, has been elegantly pleated across its width on the right arm, then thrown backwards over the left shoulder.

24. — One can see here the appearance of the pleated end hanging down behind. The whole of the draped costume is held in place by a silk cord, worn diagonally across the body, which maintains everything in place. A light *selham* of white wool muslin may then be thrown over the shoulders.

DETAILS OF FEMALE URBAN DRESS — PLATE D

1 to 3. — Different shapes of *qfatène* (sing.: *qaftane*). Of oriental origin, the *qaftane* has undergone a number of changes in shape, especially over the past thirty years.

1. — Showing the ancient cut with very wide bell-shaped sleeves. This *qaftane* did not button. It was decorated with a double row of buttons down to the waist. It was generally made of velvet, decorated with wide gold braid and frogging (see Plate 15), but it might also be of richly brocaded material. This *qaftane* still forms part of the costume of many brides. It is always worn over another *qaftane*.

2. — One can see here the shape of the cut which might be called «transitional», with straight sleeves of moderate size. This model was worn by almost all women about ten years ago. It may equally well be cut from a heavily over-decorated material, as from a perfectly ordinary one.

3. — *Qaftane* called *jabadour*, or modern cut, inspired by the male garment. This *qaftane* is cut from a thin cloth in a delicate colour and is decorated with braid of the same shade. It is very convenient to wear under the modern *jellaba*, which more and more women are adopting. All sleeved garments, whether of men or of women, have undergone changes analogous to those shown by these three shapes of *qfatène*.

4. — *Rejlin as seroual*, a sort of unfitted legging, which falls in accordeon pleats over the ankles so as to hide them (see Plate 6).

5. — *Tahtiya*, tunic whose sleeves of light muslin are embroidered on the inner surface, so that they can be turned back on the forearm (see Plate 8).

6. — *Dfina*, an over-garment of transparent material intended to soften the brilliance of the colours of the *qaftane* (see Plates 8, 9, 12).

7. — Modern townswoman wearing the *jellaba*, a piece of clothing borrowed from the male wardrobe, which is tending more and more to replace the classic *haïk*.

8 and 9. — Two models of *chrabil* (the pair: *cherbil*), velvet slippers embroidered with gold or silver thread over a cardboard base.

10. — Slipper with a thick sole and a high heel peculiar to Marrakesh and corresponding to a recent fashion, which tends to imitate the high heels of European shoes.

11. — *Qouaqeb*, a kind of little clog made from a simple wooden sole held on by a leather strap.

12. — *Rihiyya* (pl.: *rihiyyat*), a black sandal which is worn with the back part of the heel raised (a type worn particularly by the women of Rabat and Salé).

13. — Hairstyle of a young girl: two plaits, to which she can attach decorations such as ribbons, tassels, etc., hang down at the back.

14. — *Zif*, hairstyle of a young unmarried girl: cotton headscarf, generally white, enveloping the hanging plaits.

15. — Hairstyle called *chedda ed djaja* (chicken-style headdress). A modern hairstyle using an imported silk headscarf, the fringes of which are thought to look like a chicken's wings.

16. — Hairstyle called *chedda el mrouha* (fan-style headdress). So called from the large quantities of fringes which spread out on either side of the head.

It should be pointed out that hairstyles change continually following transitory fashions, which lead to frequent variations.

DETAILS OF BERBER COSTUME — PLATE E1

1 to 13. — Some examples of the most typical Berber sandals.

1. — *Loqchini*, leather sandals with a very high piece rising at the back of the heel worn in the Anti-Atlas by the Ida ou Kensous and the Ida ou Nadif (see Plate 40 and 41).

2. — *Loqchini*, model especially widespread among the Aït Abd Allah (see Plate 42); a similar form is called *idoukan* among the Issafène.

3. — Type of sandal decorated with coloured leather motifs peculiar to the Aït Atta and very common throughout the Dadès region.

4. — *Riekhit*, sandal worn by the women of the valley of the Wadi Akka.

5. — Very plain type of sandal made of leather and found very commonly throughout the whole Berber countryside. Depending on the region, they are called *cherbil* (Arabic), *iferas* (pl.: *iferoussen*), *tibouriksin* (Berber).

6. — *Nala* (pl.: *nail*), the sandal of the nomads of the south, often imported from Mauritania. The simplest type, called *tourziin*, is held on solely by a thong which passes between the big toe and the second toe (see Plate 31).

7. — Sandal consisting of a sole of dried hide held on to the foot by means of a system of cords made from dwarf palm (doum) fibre. This model is found with certain variations in form among all the mountain shepherds under different names: *irkassen* (Atlas), *tisila ourhous* (Aït Jellidasen) (see Plates 17 and 27).

8 and 9. — The kind of sandal called *rihiyya* (in Arabic) or *ikourbin* (in Berber) which is widespread in the southern part of the Atlas, the valley of the Dadès and the northern area of the Anti-Atlas. The decoration is extremely elegant: carefully worked embroidery picked out in silver thread, the designs being geometric and always worked within a lozenge (see Plate 34).

10. — *Ijekjad*, sock with a sole worn by the Aït Ouaouzguit, woven in a single piece on the loom and then sewn and reinforced with tanned sheep-skin.

11. — *Taberbasht*, decorative sandal from the Middle Atlas much used by the Aït Mguild, among whom it is also known as *sbaïd* (see Plate 19 and commentary).

12. — *Tameskhert*, another model from the Middle Atlas with a similar kind of decoration, worn by the Zaïan, Aït Sgougou, Marmoucha, Aït Serrhouchène, etc. and called either *tameskhert* or *tamnekecht*.

13. — *Isgorren*, a more solid kind of leather sandal also worn in the Middle Atlas.

14 to 18. — Method of draping the Berber man's *haïk*.

14. — Draping in the Chaouïa manner (see Plate 16). One end is placed on the left shoulder; the *haïk* is brought over the head; it then comes back forwards under the right arm.

15. — The remainder of the *haïk* is taken backwards a second time over the shoulders.

16. — The end is tossed backward so that it hangs down the back.

17. — Method of draping of the Ouaouzguit (see Plate 48 and commentary). In certain regions, for example in the Ouaouzguit territory, the length of woollen material which constitutes the *haïk* may be longer (up to 5.75 metres). This allows a more thorough envelopment of the body. One can see here the powerful anchoring role performed by the cord slung diagonally across the body from which hangs the dagger, the classic *koummiya*.

18. — The *haïk* is long enough to go over the head a second time and hang down on the right.

19. — *Qchaba* or *deréa*, a garment of the extreme south (see Plates 49, 50 and commentary). The luxury model shown here, decorated with fine embroidery is imported from Timbuktu. It is sometimes worn in southern Morocco by the sedentary peoples.

20. — *Aqcheb* (dimunitive of *qchaba*), a sleeveless woollen garment with decorative stripes, woven like the *tamizart* of the Berber women. It fastens at the shoulder, like the *tchamir*. It is in common use in the Meknes region and has been adopted in the towns by the butcher's corporation.

21. — *Jellaba* of the Rif (see Plate 18).

22. — *Azabour*, ancient model of satchel from the Rif (see Plate 18 and commentary), decorated with coloured motifs in leather, tooled and embroidered.

23. — *Akrab*, classic pattern of the satchel of the Aït Morrhad, also very widespread among neighbouring tribes.

24 to 27. — Different types of summer hat made from reed, dwarf palm (doum) fibre or esparto grass, and which is generally called *taraza* (*chemrourou* in the north). No. 24 shows the shape usually worn in the north, where it is sometimes embellished, as among the Zemmour, with numerous pompoms and embroidery (see Plate 24). The other models are from the south; in no. 27 (from the Haouz of Marrakesh) the shape of the broad-brimmed hat, petasus, worn by the ancient Greeks, is very clearly recognizable.

28. — Belt in common use throughout the whole of the Berber area of Morocco and called *hzam* (Arabic). This belt is very often used by the women in making up turbans for special occasions, thus replacing the traditional Berber *toukaït*.

29. — Another equally widespread form of belt, called *tassmert* (Anti-Atlas), *tazzebout* (Aït Ouarrain), *targouat* or *asaba* (Dra valley), the cord and the tassels varying in thickness and colour according to the tribe. The cord may go up to three or four times round the waist.

30. — *Rezza* from the south, called *iqouerzi* (Dra valley) or *taherant* (Aït Morrhad) made of fine linen twisted like a rope to form a bulky turban.

31 and 32. — Details of the headdress of the Aït Morrhad (see Plate 28). No. 32 shows the dressed hair further embellished by a turban set widthways, an arrangement peculiar to the mountain sub-divisions of the tribe.

33. — Hairstyle of the Imerrhane (see Plate 34). Silver coins or the ornaments called *tichgagalin* are fastened to the ends of the plaits.

34. — Hairstyle of the Aït Atta of the Sahara, worn in the Middle Dadès valley (see Plate 33 and commentary).

35. — The hairstyle of the Aït Serrhouchène. The bulk of the hair is plaited and falls down the back, held by a headscarf, *qtib* or *tassebnit*, bound round by cords to form a turban, *abouqs*. It is always arranged so as to form a little peak at the front. With a few variations, this is the headdress of nearly all the Berber women of the Middle Atlas.

36. — Hairstyle peculiar to the little girls of the Dadès region. The head is half shaved; a knot of hair left at the side is adorned with ornaments in the form of little round bells called *tirkhoulilin*.

37. — *Tikouyat*, a bonnet in the form of a hood worn by the little girls of the northern part of the Anti-Atlas up until their marriage. It is of blue *khent*, embroidered in a long running stitch using bright colours. A similar little hood is worn by the children in the southern part of the Anti-Atlas, particularly at Tiznit.

38. — Hairstyle of the Issafène known as *taggourt* (see Plate 43 and commentary) embellished by a silver ornament, *makhmoussa*.

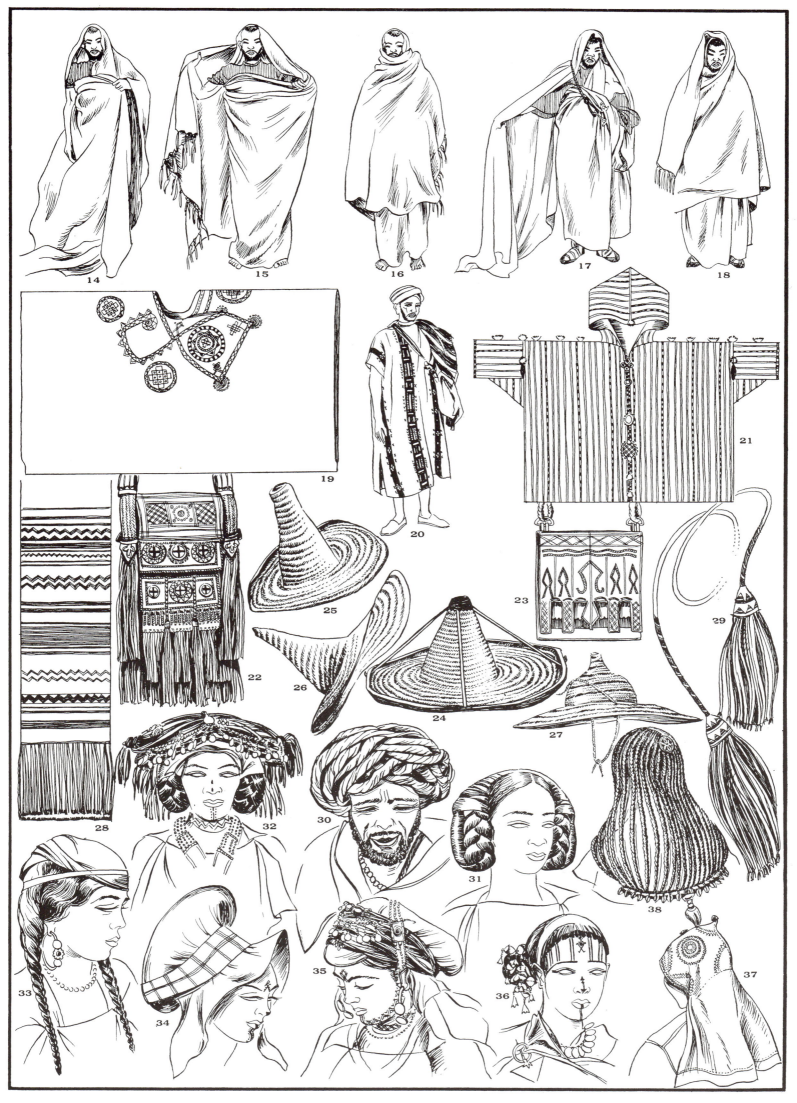

DETAILS OF JEWISH COSTUME — PLATE F

1 to 4. — Components of the Jewish bride's costume from the *mellahs* of Rabat and Salé, known as *keswa el kbira* (Plate 51).

1. — *Zeltita* (which winds around), a sort of wrap-over skirt, whose fullness is increased by three gores *(khrat)*. The decoration on the sides is a distortion of the good luck sign, *khmamès*.

2. — Bodice known as *rombaïz*, fastened in front with seven filigree buttons.

3. — Short sleeve seen from behind.

4. — Detail of the sleeve, *kmam tchmira*, spread out. Slid up over the arm, this sleeve is worn turned back onto the shoulder and attached at the back (see sketch no. 5).

5. — *Keswa el kbira* seen from behind. The two sleeves are pinned to the back; the ends of the *fechtoul* reach down to the heels.

6. — After the marriage ceremony, the *keswa el kbira* remains the feast day costume for the rest of the woman's life. Over this dress, elderly women still wear the large old-fashioned white shawl with fringes, *pagnouelo*.

7. — Detail of the *soualef*, the wig worn by the Jewish women of Rabat and Salé. The false hair is made of threads of black silk attached to a rigid band of cloth, *sfifa*, covered with three strips of gold braid. The two plaits hang down in front of the shoulders (see Plate 51).

8. — Jewish headdress from Marrakesh and Mogador. In the towns of the South, the *keswa el kbira* is again found, but the headdress does not include false hair. The real hair is hidden under the big scarf, *fechtoul*, which another silk scarf, *qtib*, covers in its turn; it is bound very tightly and worn tipped over to one side.

9. — Detail of the *soualef* worn at Fez and at Sefrou (see Plate 52). The false hair, made of silk or wool threads, here goes right round to the back of the head and hangs down without being plaited.

10. — Detail of the ancient-style *soualef* worn by the Jewish women of Todrha (see Plate 58). The false hair is made from cows' tails divided into two broad bands to which are attached two thick skeins of wool, *groune* (the horns) (see Plate 55).

11. — Hairstyle of the Jewish women of the Tafilelt (see Plate 55). It can be seen how the hanks of wool, *groune*, are tightly knotted in position and kept horizontal before being covered by the *bniqa*, a bonnet of embroidered or brocaded material.

12. — Hairstyle of the Jewish women of Goulmima (see Plate 57). The *groune* here consist of two rolls of wool which fall behind the shoulders.

13. — *Deréa*, embroidered blouse worn by the Jewish women of the Tafilelt (see Plate 55). The sleeves are worn turned back to the shoulder and the embroideries, which are on the inner surface, then become visible.

14. — Bodice worn by the Jewish women of Berguent. This garment, like the *deréa* of the Tafilelt and the costume of the young bridegroom of Erfoud (see Plate 56), is reminiscent of the folk tradition of the Balkans. The embroidery of the oldest examples is executed in cross stitch and in twisted stem stitch. The most usual colour combinations are: red and black on a white ground, green and yellow on a red ground, and green and red on a white ground.

15. — Woman of Berguent wearing an embroidered bodice with a traditional full skirt, *saya*, decorated with a little frill.

16. — Jewish woman from Tahala in her everyday dress. She is wearing the ordinary skirt, *saya*, and the bodice known as *bata* in the northern towns and as *qaftane* in the Anti-Atlas. The jewels and the wig are the same as those of Tiznit (see Plate 53).

17. — Typical urban Jewish merchant. He is wearing the *yalak*, an over-garment which replaces the *joukha* with a more opulent costume. The belt, *kerzia*, is here being worn «Tangiers-style», in other words on top of the *seroual*.

18. — Detail of the *joukha*, a kind of overall with two large pockets at the sides (see Plate 54).

19. — Detail of the *yalak*, which generally replaces the *joukha* in the feast day dress (see sketch no. 17).

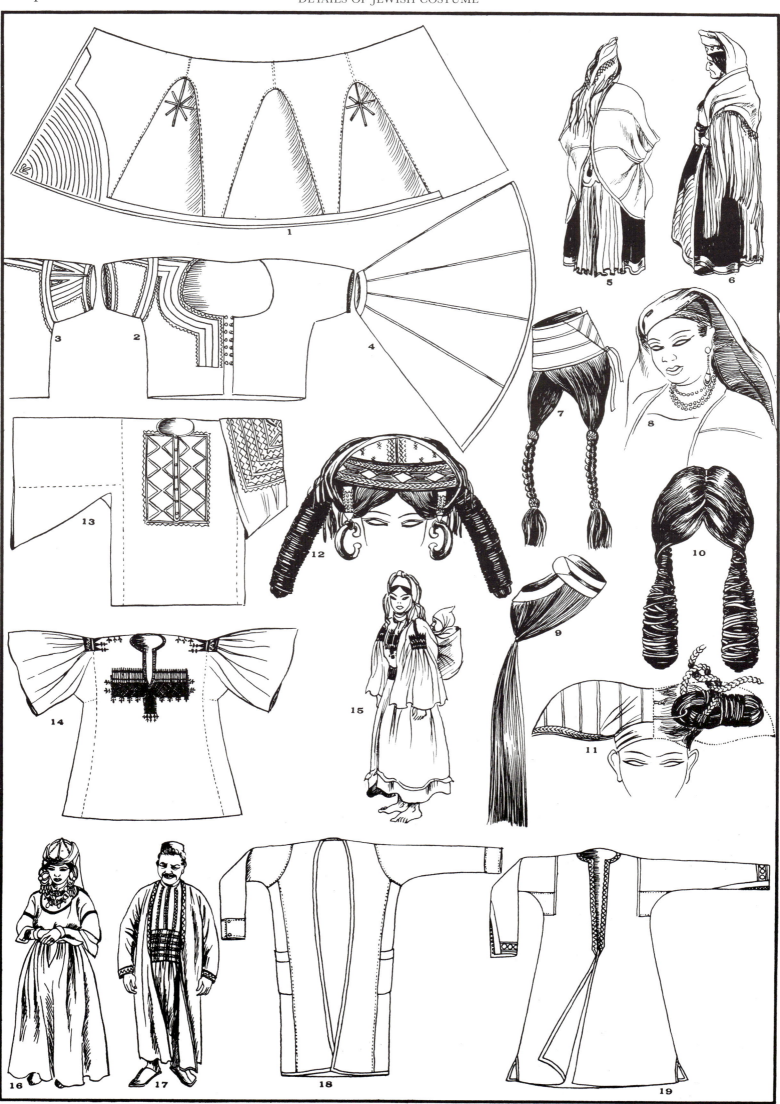

As a rule, Arab urban jewellery is made of gold. Those pieces which are not made of this noble metal are at least gilded, but there are a few exceptions, notably at Mogador where traditionally the craftsmen work in silver. Most of the urban jewels are embellished with large quantities of gems and precious stones, among which the pale rubies, known as rubies of Fez, and emeralds predominate. In the absence of such luxury materials, false stones are used to brighten up inexpensive jewellery. The pieces made today are always lighter and engraved with bastardized patterns. They are generally overloaded with little diamond rosettes, a glittery effect being desired above all else. They are then called *chibani* (old) because of the whiteness of the diamonds.

Antique pieces have become very rare and it is difficult to establish any methodical classification of them. It is, however, possible to determine at least approximately the provenance of an item of jewellery from its appearance. It is the northern towns, Tétouan, Meknes and above all Fez, which have provided the most important centres of craftsmen. These are mostly Jews who work using a variety of techniques. The jewellery from Tétouan is the most elegant, decorated with real pearls in addition to the usual gemstones (no. 21); that of Meknes tends towards rather simple geometric forms, often set off with enamels (nos. 10, 17, 20, 23); that from Fez, comprising a lot of open-work, has a more delicate, more refined character (nos. 11, 22, 26). All have visibly retained the stamp of Spanish influence. The so frequently found flower form in which a stone is set (nos. 8, 21, 22, 26, etc.) even now still bears the name *rarnati* (of Granada).

1. — *Taj* (p.: *tijan*), diadem in the antique manner. There are five major elements composed of gemstones set in gold. Depending on the model, these elements may be mounted on a hinged support, or simply set on a bed of baroque pearls sewn on to a backing made from several thicknesses of cloth (see Plates 10, 13, 15 and commentary).

2. — *Taj*, also called *touij*. The modern form of diadem worn for great occasions. It is entirely in worked gold, fitted with hinges, or sometimes with a single central hinge (Plate 12 and commentary).

3. — *Taj*, also called *akkaz*, peculiar to Fez (see Plate 11). It marks the transition between the old diadems and those which are made today.

4 and 5. — Details of the roundels, *fecha* (pl.: *fchayech*) which decorate the band, *ayyacha*, which rests on the forehead.

6. — *Khit er rih* (lit.: the thread of the wind). This is the Algerian *khit er roh* (the thread of the soul), recently imported into Morocco. It encircles the forehead like the *ayyacha* and may also be mounted on a band (see Plate 12).

7-8 and 9. — Examples of *taba* (pl.: *touaba*) a jewel which hangs on the forehead. Nos. 7 and 8 show in natural size some ancient types; no. 9 is a modern type, light with guilloche decoration, embellished with diamond rosettes which, together with its pendants, measures about 12 centimetres.

10. — Antique pendant from Meknes, embellished with enamels.

11. — Antique pendant in the form of a hand known as *khamsa* (lit.: five) or *keff*, a lucky charm which offers protection from the evil eye.

12. — Another type of *khamsa* — in some of the larger examples, the shape of the fingers may be so stylized that they are no longer apparent; the jewel is then known as *louha* (lit.: small board).

13. — *Foulet khamsa* (bean with five grains), jewel with the same property of bringing good luck.

14. — *Rabouz* (bellows) or *qalb* (heart), filigree pendant.

15 and 16. — Patterns of brooches: *chouka et teyr* (bird brooch) and *kummiya* (dagger). The brooch is an item recently introduced into the Moroccan woman's jewellery. As a consequence the motifs represented frequently break with tradition. They may be stylized versions of the most modern objects, e.g.: *chouka et tiyara* (aeroplane brooch). Let us mention in passing that the Moroccan woman may also wear attached to her person a little watch, *magana*, containing the portrait of the Sultan.

17 to 19. — Pendants of the *lebba* (pl.: *lebbat*), a very large antique necklace composed of seven or nine similar pendants joined together by gold balls, which may be smooth, of filigree or faceted, called *krakeb* (see Plates 10, 12, 13). These pendants are here shown natural size.

20 to 24. — Rosettes of the *tazra* (pl.: *tazrat*), an antique form of necklace composed of three large rosettes, each of which may have a radius of up to 8 or 9 centimetres, linked together by gold balls or by various other motifs (see Plates 14 and 15). Nos. 20, 21 and 22 are, respectively, typical examples of the art of the jewellers of Meknes, Tétouan and Fez.

25. — *Fnar* (pl.: *fnarat*) (lantern), pendants some 20 centimetres in length which are attached at the temples and hang down on either side of the face (see Plate 13). A very old ornament peculiar to Meknes, to be compared to the *kandila* of Tunisia, whose name means lamp.

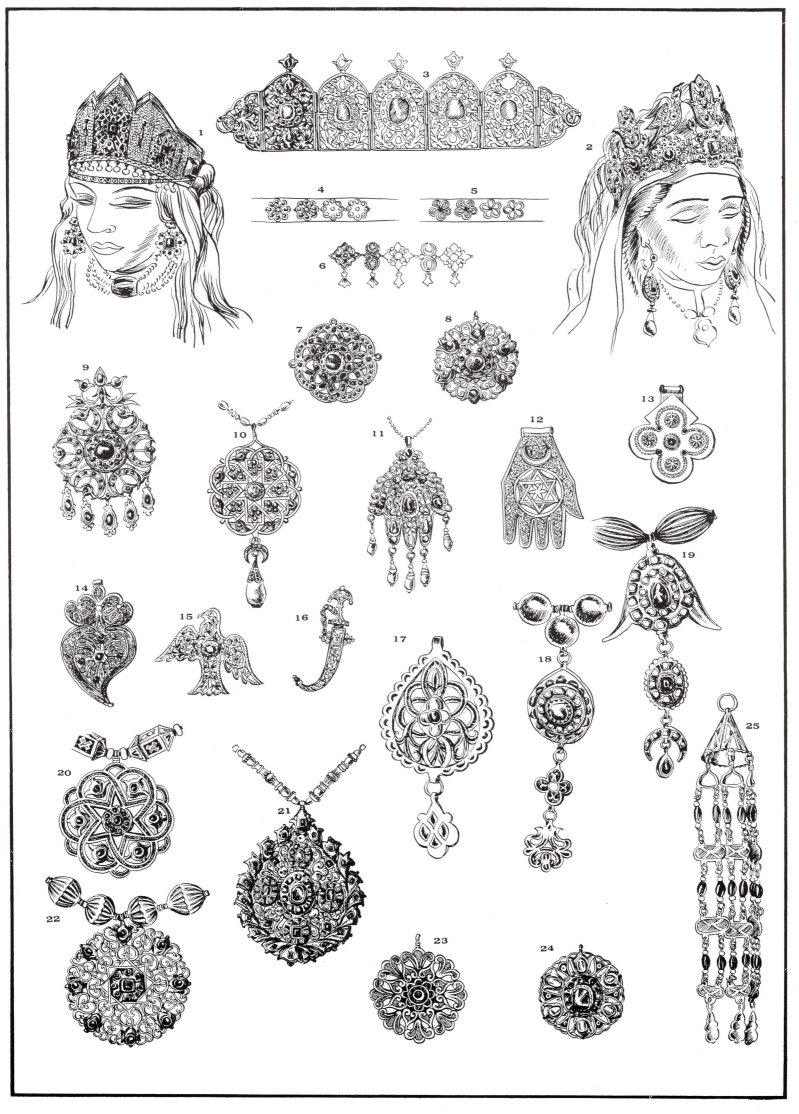

26. — Antique type of earring in use particularly in Tangiers and Fez. They were supported by a little chain and hook attached to the headdress and were called *khras kbach* (ram's head earrings) or else *khras amara* (very heavily worked earrings) because of their very elaborate decoration.

27. — *Douah*, large rings with five coral pendants which were in very common use at Rabat, but were above all worn in Marrakesh. The big complete rings, more ordinary, are called *mfatel*.

28. — Antique form of *aqraychat* (shrimp) earrings with three pendants worn in Fez.

29. — Modern form of *mataychat* (swings), a jewel from Fez, known in other towns as *halaqat*.

30 and 31. — Forms of the *zwaheg*, small-sized earrings.

32. — *Bziyem* (sing.: *bzim*), fibulae pinning the *izar del harir*, which is worn over ceremonial clothes.

33. — *Bziemat* (diminutive of *bziyem*), small fibulae.

34 to 39. — Various types of bracelets, *deblij* (pl.: *dbalej*).

34. — *Chems ou qmar* (sun and moon), with alternating facets of gold and silver.

35. — *Taasir saboun* (wrung-out washing), so called because of the closely set ribs which suggest linen wrung out to dry.

36. — *Deblij mkherram* (pierced bracelet).

37 and 38. — Modern shapes, solid, engraved and with guilloche decoration. When they are very thin they are called *dbalej mfrourin*. They can also be given the names of the motifs decorating them.

39. — *Slouk* (lit.: wires), very thin bands called *simana* when they are seven in number like the days of the week.

40. — *Khelkhal* (pl.: *khlakhel*), an anklet fastened by means of a pin attached to a chain.

41. — *Kelkhal* shown open.

42 and 43. — Models of belt buckles called *fekroun* (tortoise). Most of the modern ones are of gold, set with stones. These two in silver are from Mogador, where the craftsmen do their skilful engraving principally on this metal.

44 to 56. — Different kinds of rings, *khouatem* (sing.: *khatem*). There is a wide range of different patterns; these are usually named after the object which their decoration represents.

44. — *Khatem et teyr* (bird ring), an ancient pattern, originally Jewish, but also worn by Arab women.

45 and 46. — *Khatem et taj* (diadem ring). The design does in fact call to mind the ceremonial diadem called *taj*.

47. — *Khatem el ach* (bird's nest ring). The disk of the design suggests a nest containing eggs, which are represented by the stones.

48. — A type, formerly very widely distributed, in which we again find on a reduced scale the ornament called *rarnati* (from Granada) which we have already mentioned.

49. — *Khatem aïn al herr* (cat's eye ring), a ring the clear stone of which is said to represent a cat's eye, and which has a reputation for preventing sterility in women.

50. — Ring the stone of which consists of a large onyx engraved with ancient letters. The claw setting is standard.

51. — Standard setting of the modern *khatem al ach*.

52. — Another type of setting.

53. — A very widespread ancient design.

54. — Model worn by men: a bezel set signet ring.

55 and 56. — Two common models of modern ring. To keep their price within reasonable limits, these are very thin and light, with simple guilloche decoration. Their shape usually suggests either a hand, *khatem al khamsa*, a heart, *khatem al qalb*, or an almond, *khatem al louza*.

We have said in this work how much Berber jewellery varies in detail and in decoration from one region to another. I have therefore had to limit myself here to showing a few typical pieces, in particular choosing those whose structure and decoration could not be seen sufficiently clearly due to their small scale in the costume plates.

1. — *Taounza* of the Aït Serrhouchène. This diadem consists of a hook, *isernas*, which is attached at the back to the headscarf, of a system of small chains, *acherab*, which link the plates, *tillarouzin*, together and support the earrings, *tikharsiin*, at the sides, and of a main headband consisting of three elements which makes up the frontal decoration; to it are fastened the small pendants, *ahfaiden*, which hang down to the level of the eyes. The decoration of the various elements is carried out in a rudimentary form of niello-work produced with the resin of the *taqa*, which is run while hot into the engraved channels. This diadem is found, with a few variants, among the Aït Youssi, the Marmoucha and some of the Aït Ouarrain. It is also very similar to the *taounza* worn in the Anti-Atlas (see Plate 40).

2 and 3. — *Tikharsiin*, flat earrings supported by the *acherab*. Only the outer surface is decorated (same geographical distribution as the *taounza*).

4. — *Tiknouchin*, a piece of jewellery of the Aït Serrhouchène. Ornaments which hang over the temples and consist of little dished disks, held in place by a ring on the inner surface and also embellished with *ahfaiden*. This jewel is found under different names as far as the Atlas, among the Aït Morrhad (see Plate 28) and even in the valleys of the Dadès and of the Dra, where it is most commonly used as a pendant of the fibula (see Plate 60).

5. — *Talgamout* (lit.: the little bit), a head ornament smaller in size than the *taounza*. The whole arrangement of small chains and hooks for the sides and back can be seen. This pattern is that worn by the Imerrhane (see Plate 34). There are a great variety of them in the Anti-Atlas, as far as Tiznit, where it is known as *tassibba*. An ornament made exclusively of small chains called *rfadet* is also worn in the Atlas and in particular among the Aït Morrhad, who call it *assensir*.

The standard *tasfift*, a diadem which goes round the upper part of the forehead and which is met more or less everywhere under different shapes and names, completes the range of head ornaments, properly so-called.

6. — *Tassarit* (fragment), a necklace of niello-work pendants embellished with cabochons of which there is a great variety in the oases of the south of the Anti-Atlas.

The tribes of the Anti-Atlas and its pre-Saharan oases are especially rich in jewels. The Berbers call them, in a general way, jewels of the Souss. This term should not be taken to mean the basin of the Souss proper, but rather all the territories of the former «kingdom of Souss», which in fact stretched a very long way south. These pieces of jewellery are among the most interesting in Morocco. Some Spanish influence can be detected, which may perhaps be due to Andalusian craftsmen having formed, in the course of their emigration of long ago, isolated nuclei where certain techniques have been preserved.

In the same way, similarities with Sudanese jewellery are sometimes apparent. In this latter case, it may reasonably be assumed that the Muslims of the Saadian period left the mark of their influence on the craftsmen of the black countries which they long held under their rule, rather than their having drawn inspiration from so primitive an environment.

In addition to a very wide variety of local names, the general name of the necklace, *tazra*, is very widespread throughout the whole Berber area of Morocco.

7. — An ancient *tazra* of the Glaoua (fragment). In the Glaoua country, examples of the old pieces of jewellery made by the skilled craftsmen of the Ouaouzguit region, whose techniques are related to those of the jewellers of the Souss, can still be found. In the old necklaces, the great spherical beads decorated with filigree work or with cloisonné enamel, called *tagemmout* or *tagmoust*, are as important as the pendants worked in the same way. These elements, while similar in general outline, vary continually from one to another in the details of their decoration. The technique by which they are made and their individuality, bear witness to the richness of a folk tradition now firmly on the road to disappearance.

To these necklaces, should be added the whole range of coral necklaces and, above all, those of amber called *loubane* and *talloubane* (see Plates 29, 40, 45, 57, etc.)

8. — *Tikhorsin*, earrings worn by the *hartaniat* of the middle valley of the Dra (see Plate 37). This kind of earring (7 to 8 centimetres with the pendants) is the most widespread kind in Berber country, the type of pendants varying from region to region.

9. — *Ddouh*, heavy earrings made by the jewellers of the *mellah* of Tahala. Nine pendants make these earrings decorated with cabochons and enamels even heavier, and they are supported by a little chain going over the head. These earrings are worn by the Jewish women of the *mellahs* of the Anti-Atlas, as well as by the Chleuh women of Tiznit and the surrounding countryside (see Plate 46). Their weight is enormous, but, as is also the case with the rings from Todrha, called *talhourset*, which weigh close to 400 grams (see Plates 57 and 58), the Jewish women do not usually hang the ring from the ear itself. It is noteworthy, however, that the Berbers frequently make a large hole in the ear lobe to take the ring and when this is not in place, the hole is kept open by means of a plug.

10. — *Tikhoursin* (outer surface and profile), earrings from the Anti-Atlas, made and worn by the Ida ou Nadif and the Ida ou Kensous.

11. — *Tikhoursin ougelnin*, earrings from the same region (see Plates 40 and 41). Very large in size, these earrings, together with their supporting hook, may reach a length of 20 centimetres.

12 to 18. — Typical patterns of bracelets.

12. — *Azbi n'iqourraïn*, a massive moulded bracelet with twelve points, worn in the far south and especially by the women of the Aït Atta (see Plate 29 and commentary).

13. — *Adeblij* (pl.: *adblijan*) (name of Arabic origin), pattern of bracelet with angular points made at Tahala. This kind of bracelet is also found in the Atlas (Aït Hadiddou) and in the Middle Atlas (Aït Serrhouchène).

14. — *Meufokh*, a bracelet with studded raised decoration from south of the Dra valley. This type is also found in the oases of the south-west.

15. — *Nbala* (pl.: *nbaïl*, in Arabic) or *tanbalt* (pl.: *tanballin*, in Berber), a large hinged bracelet closed by a pin. This model from Tahala is much worn at Tiznit (see Plate 46). A bracelet of the same type, but decorated using local techniques, is found in the Middle Atlas (Zaïan, Marmoucha, Aït Youssi, etc.).

16. — *Azbeg* (pl.: *ibzgan*), an open bracelet. This model comes from the Aït Serrhouchène, but the same kind of bracelet is found, with local decoration, in the Souss and in the south of the Anti-Atlas as well as in the Atlas, in particular among the Aït Hadiddou, where it is known as *azebj* (pl.: *izebjane n'aït imaoum*). It is, in principle, a bracelet for young unmarried girls.

17. — A massive bracelet with big decorative ribs widespread throughout the Moroccan South, called *Azbi* by the Aït Atta. When it is not plain, its decoration is very simple — a few roughly nielloed grooves. Women often wear a pair on each wrist. They reach their maximum weight in the Todrha (nearly 500 grams) and there each pair is separated by a little washer of leather, *tabouqs* (see Plate 32 and commentary).

18. — *Adeblij*, pattern found throughout the Middle Atlas.

19 and 20. — Patterns of *ikhalkhalen* (sing.: *khelkhal*), anklets. No. 19 is a model from the Atlas. No. 20, which has faceted ends, is a type very widespread throughout the Middle Atlas and eastern Morocco and is called *khelkhal mebroum*. These two models are decorated with small punched motifs.

21 to 26. — Typical patterns of the fibulae used to pin together the *izar*.

21. — The most classic pattern, which is found with a few variations throughout the whole Berber country with the usual local names. The decoration is moulded or engraved.

22. — The pattern called *tizerzay*, of enormous size, worn in the oases of the south-west. It is engraved and lightly pierced; some are entirely covered with tiny open-work holes.

23. — Pattern of *khelalat* (Arabic), peculiar to the Jewish women of the Todrha. A convex silver disk, comparable to the *tiknouchin* of the Aït Serrhouchène, is often added to it as a pendant.

24. — Triangular pattern used by the Glaoua, which carries, as well as the usual chain linking the two fibulae, a hollow pendant, *herz*, in which are placed short extracts of verses from the Koran.

25. — Pattern of the Zaän, called *tisernas*, with a hollow pear-shaped pendant, called *lanibra* or *beurnil*, to which is attached five little chains carrying small coins.

26. — Pattern used by the Aït Serrhouchène. A type of fibula made in a mould, the relief decoration of which is in consequence less crisp than when engraved.

27 to 38. — Typical patterns for rings, the generic name of which is *khouatem* (in Arabic) or *takhaten* (in Berber).

27-28 and 29. — Models common in the Middle Atlas.

30. — Pattern with little pendants used among the Aït Serrhouchène and the Marmoucha and regarded as a wedding ring.

31-32 and 33. — Models from the Anti-Atlas much esteemed at Tiznit. The decoration consists of yellow, green and turquoise blue enamel separated by filigree work.

34. — Semi-filigree model with a large pointed bezel similar to certain rings from the Sudan, which are to be found in the oases of the Ferkla and of the Tafilelt. The Jewish women thread them on plaited cords to make ornaments for their headdresses.

35. — Chased pattern from the Atlas.

36. — Semi-filigree pattern, of Sudanese influence, very widespread in the oases of the south-west.

37. — Classic model from the Ida ou Nadif, decorated with a great red cabochon.

38. — A very light model of ring with a thin round disk soberly decorated in niello-work, extremely common at Tagmout. All these models from the south and in particular this last, threaded on plaited cords, make up the diadems in general use among the women of the oases of the south-west, diadems which are in fact simply known as *khouatem*.

N.B. The drawings in this book and their commentaries are intended to provide supplementary information. They do not necessarily represent all the most uncommon details and preference has been given to certain objects not shown in the plates and to those which cannot be seen clearly because of the smallness of the scale.